CAMBRIDGE LI

Books of en

Polar Exploration

This series includes accounts, by eye-witnesses and contemporaries, of early expeditions to the Arctic and the Antarctic. Huge resources were invested in such endeavours, particularly the search for the North-West Passage, which, if successful, promised enormous strategic and commercial rewards. Cartographers and scientists travelled with many of the expeditions, and their work made important contributions to earth sciences, climatology, botany and zoology. They also brought back anthropological information about the indigenous peoples of the Arctic region and the southern fringes of the American continent. The series further includes dramatic and poignant accounts of the harsh realities of working in extreme conditions and utter isolation in bygone centuries.

The Possibility of Approaching the North Pole Asserted

Daines Barrington (1727/8–1800) and Mark Beaufoy (1764–1827) became fellows of the Royal Society in 1767 and 1790 respectively. Barrington's contributions to the *Philosophical Transactions* favoured natural history, but another of his passions was polar exploration and a potential sea route through the Arctic Ocean. Beaufoy, an astronomer and physicist, was notably involved in discerning changes in the earth's magnetic field. Reissued in their 1818 second edition, these papers discuss Arctic exploration and evidence for the theorised open polar sea. Barrington's tracts, originally dating from the 1770s, draw on the testimony of those navigators who had ventured into high latitudes. Though flawed, his hopes of explorers pushing through the pack ice retain considerable historical interest. A map of the North Pole and the surrounding region, so far as it was known, is included. The appendix contains Beaufoy's papers from 1817, including questions answered by Russians who wintered on Spitsbergen.

Cambridge University Press has long been a pioneer in the reissuing of out-of-print titles from its own backlist, producing digital reprints of books that are still sought after by scholars and students but could not be reprinted economically using traditional technology. The Cambridge Library Collection extends this activity to a wider range of books which are still of importance to researchers and professionals, either for the source material they contain, or as landmarks in the history of their academic discipline.

Drawing from the world-renowned collections in the Cambridge University Library and other partner libraries, and guided by the advice of experts in each subject area, Cambridge University Press is using state-of-the-art scanning machines in its own Printing House to capture the content of each book selected for inclusion. The files are processed to give a consistently clear, crisp image, and the books finished to the high quality standard for which the Press is recognised around the world. The latest print-on-demand technology ensures that the books will remain available indefinitely, and that orders for single or multiple copies can quickly be supplied.

The Cambridge Library Collection brings back to life books of enduring scholarly value (including out-of-copyright works originally issued by other publishers) across a wide range of disciplines in the humanities and social sciences and in science and technology.

The Possibility of Approaching
the North Pole Asserted

DAINES BARRINGTON
EDITED BY MARK BEAUFOY

CAMBRIDGE
UNIVERSITY PRESS

CAMBRIDGE
UNIVERSITY PRESS

University Printing House, Cambridge, CB2 8BS, United Kingdom

Published in the United States of America by Cambridge University Press, New York

Cambridge University Press is part of the University of Cambridge.
It furthers the University's mission by disseminating knowledge in the pursuit of
education, learning and research at the highest international levels of excellence.

www.cambridge.org
Information on this title: www.cambridge.org/9781108071840

© in this compilation Cambridge University Press 2014

This edition first published 1818
This digitally printed version 2014

ISBN 978-1-108-07184-0 Paperback

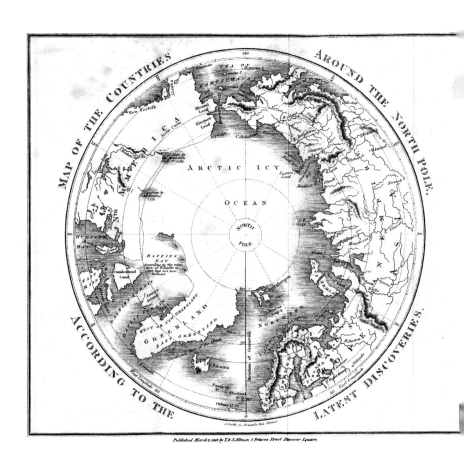

The material originally positioned here is too large for reproduction in this reissue. A PDF can be downloaded from the web address given on page iv of this book, by clicking on 'Resources Available'.

THE

POSSIBILITY

OF

APPROACHING THE NORTH POLE

ASSERTED.

BY

THE HON. D. BARRINGTON.

A NEW EDITION.

WITH

AN APPENDIX,

CONTAINING

PAPERS ON THE SAME SUBJECT,

AND ON

𝕬 𝕹𝖔𝖗𝖙𝖍 𝖂𝖊𝖘𝖙 𝕻𝖆𝖘𝖘𝖆𝖌𝖊.

BY

COLONEL BEAUFOY, F.R.S.

ILLUSTRATED WITH A MAP OF THE NORTH POLE, ACCORDING TO THE LATEST DISCOVERIES.

SECOND EDITION.

W. M. Craig, del.   Berryman, sc.

LONDON:

PRINTED FOR T. AND J. ALLMAN,

PRINCES STREET, HANOVER SQUARE;

W. H. REID, CHARING CROSS; AND BALDWIN, CRADOCK, AND JOY,

PATERNOSTER ROW.

1818.

PREFACE.

————

THE interesting nature of the subject
to which the following Papers relate,
would, at any time, justify their republication; but at the present moment they
derive an additional value from the expedition which is now preparing to explore
the Arctic Regions. Whether the extended
boundaries of geographical science, aided
by the local information which it is said
has been communicated by those who are
employed in the Greenland Fisheries, will
secure the success of this enterprise, it is
impossible to anticipate; but, as English-

men, we must naturally wish, that discoveries, which were first attempted by the
adventurous spirit and maritime skill of
our countrymen, should be finally achieved
by the same means.

As early as the year 1527, the idea of
a passage to the East Indies by the North
Pole was suggested by a Bristol Merchant
to Henry VIII; but no voyage seems to
have been undertaken for the purpose of
navigating the Circumpolar Seas till the
commencement of the following century,
when, in 1607, an expedition was fitted
out, at the expense of certain Merchants
of London. To this attempt several
others succeeded at different periods, and
all of them were projected and carried
into execution by private individuals.
The adventurers did not indeed accom-

plish the object they exclusively sought, that of reaching India by a nearer route than doubling the Cape of Good Hope; but though they failed in that respect, the fortitude, perseverance, and skill which they manifested, exhibited the most irrefragable proofs of the early existence of that superiority in naval affairs, which has progressively elevated this country to her present eminence among the nations of Europe.

At length, after the lapse of above a century and a half, this interesting question became an object of royal patronage, and the expedition which was commanded by Captain Phipps, afterwards Lord Mulgrave, in 1773, was fitted out at the charge of Government. It will add to the value of the following pages when

it is known, that the author of them
was the first proposer of this memorable
voyage ; and that, in consequence of his
representations, as to the practicability
of circumnavigating the Pole, the Royal
Society made that application to Lord
Sandwich, then at the head of the Admiralty, which led to the appointment of
the expedition for exploring those regions.

Though Captain Phipps found it impossible to penetrate the wall of ice, which
extended for more than twenty degrees
between the latitudes of 80° and 81°, the
opinions of Mr. Barrington, upon the
possibility of proceeding farther, under
different circumstances, remained un-
shaken.   With indefatigable assiduity
therefore he began to collect every fact

connected with the subject ; and as he
accumulated his materials he read them
to the Royal Society. This mass of
written, traditionary, and conjectural evidence, he afterwards published, in the
year 1775 ; and it cannot be denied that
its republication at the present moment is
at least appropriate, independently of the
intrinsic value which must always attach
to the researches of so acute and ardent
an inquirer.

The Publishers, however, are happy in
being permitted to add to the value of
these Tracts, by subjoining, as an Appendix, some Papers upon the same subject
by Colonel Beaufoy, F.R.S. The attention of that gentleman was turned to the
practicability of reaching the North Pole,
from Spitzbergen, during winter, by tra-

velling over the ice and snow in sledges drawn by rein deer. He therefore transmitted various queries, to which he received answers from Russians who had wintered in those remote islands. The information thus elicited is exceedingly curious, and much of it may be most advantageously employed by those who are about to brave the dangers and inclemencies of that dreary climate.

In order to render the present volume as complete as possible, an entirely new Map of the North Pole is prefixed, drawn from the best authorities, and with the Pole in the centre, so as to exhibit the utmost degree of latitude which has hitherto been approached. Under all these circumstances, it is hoped the Work will find a favourable reception. Its claims, indeed, are of no dubious nature ; for it is the production of persons eminent for their scientific attainments. Subsequent discoveries can alone impair its value. Till the ardour of well-directed enterprize shall disclose what yet remains unexplored, the exposition of our actual knowledge, and the speculative deductions of enlightened theory, cannot be unacceptable to the lovers of geographical research.

MARCH 1,
1818.

PREFACE

TO

THE POLAR TRACTS.

BY THE

HONOURABLE DAINES BARRINGTON.

———————

THE following Tracts, relative to the possibility of near approaches to the Pole of our own hemisphere, as likewise of a communication between the Atlantic and Pacific Oceans in any Northern direction, were first published in 1775 and 1776.

I now think it right again to print them, because they contain many well attested facts with regard to reaching high Northern Latitudes, which are not to be found elsewhere, and have a tendency to promote geographical discoveries. I am very ready to admit, indeed, that the purposes of commerce can never be answered by the great uncertainty of a constant passage (even when such communication is discovered), in seas which are so frequently obstructed by the ice packing in vast fields. I find likewise, that since the Resolution and Endeavour returned from their last voyage, many conceive a North East or North West Passage to be impracticable, because our ships, in two successive years, were not able to penetrate beyond 71°, by impediments of ice. Besides, however, that the ice packing in particular situations varies often in different years, both these attempts were made in the month of August, which I flatter myself to have proved, is the very season of the year when the ice, breaking up on the coast, is floating in every direction, and consequently often packs in masses of an immense extent.

These vast fields of ice, indeed, often are dispersed; but who hath, or indeed should have, the fortitude of waiting for this accident, whilst he is already in a high Northern Latitude, and the winter is fast approaching? If the ice, however, should thus pack in April or May (which I conceive it would not, as little must be left to float from the preceding summer), yet as the warm weather is then increasing from day to day, the navigator would wait with some degree of patience till his ship may be released from this temporary obstruction. The situation of the discoverer, under these circumstances, may be compared to a traveller passing over a large tract of sea sand, when the tide is flowing or ebbing. In the first instance he spurs his horse, because the sea may be expected at his heels; in the latter he proceeds with great composure, as every instant he loses in point of time the sea is farther removed.

Others again have despaired of a North West Passage, from Captain Pickersgill not having succeeded in his attempt for this purpose during the year 1776*.

This voyage was intended for two purposes (at least as I have been informed;) the first to protect some of our whale fishers on the coast of West Greenland from the Americans then in rebellion; and the second (if the time after this service permitted) to join Captain Cook, should he have been so fortunate as to have accomplished his passage from the Pacific

* In the Lion armed brig.

Ocean, when he would probably have returned to England by Davis's Straits

This plan seems to have been very well laid, but that persevering navigator was delayed at the Cape by Captain Clark's ship not arriving till a considerable time after his own reaching that place of rendezvous, and in the farther progress of his voyage by adverse winds, which drove him to the Friendly Islands instead of Otaheite, so that he did not make his attempt of a passage till 1777.

Captain Pickersgill did not leave Scilly till the 10th of June 1766, and consequently, whatever obstructions he met with from floating or packing ice, might be reasonably expected when he reached the coast of West Greenland. It appears, however, by what I shall copy from the conclusion of his Journal on the 31st of August, that he did not find these to be

b

considerable, and that after the trial his hopes of a passage were very sanguine.

" I shall conclude with a few observations on this part of the world (sc. Greenland) and so terribly represented by people, who, in order to raise their own merit, make dangers and difficulties of common occurrences, merely because the places are unknown, and there is little or no probability of their being ever contradicted. I do not mean this as a personal reflection ; but having discoursed with many of the masters of Greenland vessels as well as their employers, and heard such dreadful stories of those countries, I cannot help remarking it as tending to mislead those, who, from a laudable principle, would be benefactors to their country, but are deterred from it by these misrepresentations. I shall communicate observations on the ice, the atmosphere, the land of Forbisher, *and the probability of a North West Passage, in a short time*.*"

This, however, hath unfortunately been prevented by Captain Pickersgill's death; but the Astronomer Royal, who communicated Captain Pickersgill's Journal to the Royal Society, hath informed me by letter, " That he had often heard this navigator express himself as well assured of a North West Passage; adding, that he received accounts of it from the inhabitants on the side of Davis's Straits, and that it was directly North West, very different from Baffin's track.

" Captain Pickersgill likewise thought, that *the best method to find the passage was to get out early, before the ice broke away in the upper part of Davis's Straits.*"

* Phil. Trans. for 1778. part ii, p. 1063.

It thus appears, that the last attempts of a North West Passage ended with the officer's employed thereon being thoroughly persuaded, that it was not only practicable, but highly probable.

As the late geographical discoveries have given such general satisfaction, I have little doubt but that they will be farther prosecuted when a peace takes place, and shall therefore here venture to throw out my poor thoughts with regard to the yet remaining desiderata for the more perfect knowledge of the planet which we inhabit. When we are informed by proper trials, that the attempt in any particular direction cannot succeed, we shall then be as much at rest as with regard to Lunar oceans or continents, if such there be.

I have mentioned in the following Tracts, that the parliamentary rewards

given for approaching within one degree
of the North Pole are not likely to produce the effects intended, because the
Greenland whale ships are all ensured;
if they were therefore to go beyond the
common fishing latitudes, it would be
such a departure from the voyage ensured,
that they would not be able to recover, if
accidents happened in such a deviation.

I am informed, however, that there are
some vessels employed in time of peace by
government, to prevent smuggling on the
Northern Coast of Scotland. These ships
might be instructed, when a promising
wind blows from the Southward, to proceed as far North as the ice will permit.
The crew of such a ship would be en-
couraged by expectations of the parliamentary reward; and though one attempt
might fail, another might succeed. The
expense to the public would be trifling,

whilst the smugglers would not know how soon the ship might return to its station.

Our Commodore upon the Newfoundland station might also send a vessel, at a small expense, to explore all the Northern part of Hudson's Bay, with which we are so imperfectly acquainted at present.

Such attempts during peace might take place almost every summer; and I should suppose that this scientific and opulent nation would never hesitate (whilst there is the least dawning of hopes) to send proper vessels occasionally to make farther trials both of a North West Passage by Baffin's Bay, and a North East beyond Nova Zembla.

The coast of Corea, the Northern part of Japan, and the Lequieux Islands, should also be explored; the cheapest and perhaps best method of doing this would be to employ a vessel in the India Company's service, which might be victualled at Canton.

Thus much with regard to discoveries, or better knowledge of the more unfrequented parts of the Northern Hemisphere.

The desiderata in that of the South seem to be the following :—

To make the complete circumnavigation of New Holland, so as at least to be better acquainted with some parts of the coast of this immense island; a vessel for this purpose might be victualled at the Cape of Good Hope, or Canton : nor is the voyage a distant one, when compared with those of Captain Cook. New Guinea also should be better explored.

We scarcely know more of the islands of Tristan da Cunha than their Longitude and Latitude; but their interior parts should be examined. Not vastly distant is Sandwich Land, which many on board

Captain Cook supposed to be a vast continent. It may be objected, indeed, that if it is so, it will turn out to be a continent of ice and snow; I am not here, however, recommending discoveries for the purpose of commerce, but for the improvement of geography.

I should conceive, that a voyage either from the Cape or Brasil would easily give opportunity of effectuating both these purposes.

Perhaps, whilst discoveries by sea are thus dwelt upon, encouragement should be given to travellers by land, for procuring better information with regard to the central parts of Asia, Africa, and America. In short, let us endeavour to know as much as we may of our globe; nor should this be considered as a vain and trifling curiosity, though no benefits to commerce may result from these inquiries.

INSTANCES OF NAVIGATORS

WHO HAVE REACHED

HIGH NORTHERN LATITUDES.

———◆———

Read at a Meeting of the Royal Society,
MAY 19, 1774.

────────────

AS I was the unworthy proposer of the Voyage towards the North Pole, which the Council of the Royal Society recommended to the Board of Admiralty, I think it my duty to lay before the Society such intelligence as I have happened to procure with regard to navigators having reached high Northern Latitudes * ; because

* It is well known, that there are many such accounts in print, but to these I need not refer the Society.

B

some of these accounts seem to promise, that
we may proceed farther towards the Pole than
the very able Officers, who were sent on this
destination last year, were permitted to penetrate, notwithstanding their repeated efforts to
pass beyond $80\frac{1}{2}°$.

I shall begin, however, by making an observation or two with regard to the Greenland
Fishery, which will in a great measure account
for our not being able to procure many instances of nearer approaches to the Pole than
the Northern parts of Spitzbergen.

Fifty years ago, such apprehensions were
entertained of navigating even in the loose, or
what is called *sailing ice*, that the crews commonly continued on shore *, from whence they
only pursued the whales in boats.

The demand, however, for oil increasing,
whilst the number of fish rather decreased, they
were obliged to proceed to sea in quest of them,

* There were houses still standing on Spitzbergen, where
the Dutch used to boil their train oil --Marten's Voyage,
p. 24. See also Callander, vol. iii, p. 723.

and now by experience and adroitness seldom suffer from the obstructions of ice *.

The masters of ships, who are employed in this trade, have no other object but the catching whales, which, as long as they can procure in more Southern Latitudes, they certainly will not go in search of at a greater distance from the port to which they are to return: they, therefore, seldom proceed much beyond 80° North Latitude, unless driven by a strong Southerly Wind or other accident.

Whenever this happens, also, it is only by very diligent inquiries that any information can be procured ; for the masters, not being commonly men of science, or troubling their heads about the improvement of geographical knowledge, never mention these circumstances on their return, because they conceive that no one is more interested about these matters than they are themselves. Many of the Greenland Masters are likewise directed to return after the

---

* These particulars I received from Captain Robinson, whom I shall have hereafter occasion to mention.

early fishery is over, provided they have
tolerable success; so that they have no opportunity of making discoveries to the Northward.

To these reasons it may be added, that no
ships were perhaps ever sent before last summer
with express instructions to reach the Pole, if
possible, as most other attempts have been to
discover a North East or North West Passage,
which were soon defeated by falling in with
land, or other accident.

Having thus endeavoured to show that the
instances of ships reaching high Northern Latitudes must necessarily be rare, I shall now proceed to lay before the Society such as I have
been able to hear of since the voyage towards
the- North Pole was undertaken during last
summer.

When this was determined upon, and mentioned in the Newspapers, it became matter of
conversation amongst the crews of the guard
ships; and Andrew Leekie, an intelligent seaman on board the Albion (then stationed at

Plymouth), informed some of the officers that he had been as far North as $84\frac{1}{2}°$.

When he was asked farther on this head, he said, that he was on board the Reading, Captain Thomas Robinson, in 1766, and that, whilst he was shaving the Captain, Mr. Robinson told him, that he had probably never been so far to the Northward before, as they had now reached the above-mentioned degree of latitude.

Having happened to hear this account of Leekie's, on my return to London this winter, I found out Captain Robinson, who remembered his having had this conversation with Leekie; but said, that he was mistaken in supposing that they had reached $84\frac{1}{2}°$ North Latitude, as they were only in $82\frac{1}{2}°$.

Captain Robinson then explained himself, that he had at this time computed his latitude by the run back to Hakluyt's Headland in twenty four hours; from which, and other circumstances mentioned in my presence before two sea officers, they told me afterwards, that they had little or no doubt of the accuracy of his reckoning. Mr. Robinson likewise remembers that the sea was then open, so that he hath no doubt of being able to reach 83°, but how much farther he will not pretend to say.

This same Captain, in the ship St. George, was, on the 15th of June, 1773, in North Latitude 81° 16′, by a very accurate observation with an approved Hadley's quadrant, in which he also made the proper allowance for the refraction in high Northern Latitudes; at which time seeing some whales spouting to the Northward he pursued them for five hours, so that he must have reached $81\frac{1}{2}$, when the sea was open to the Westward and East North East as far as he could distinguish from the mast-head. His longitude was then 8° East from the meridian of London.

Captain Robinson is a very intelligent seaman, and hath navigated the Greenland Seas these twenty years, except during the interval that he was employed by the Hudson's Bay Company*.

I could add some other, perhaps interesting, particulars, which I have received from Captain Robinson, with regard to Spitzbergen and the Polar Seas; I will only mention, however, that he thinks he could spend a winter not uncomfortably in the most Northern parts we are acquainted with †, as there are three or four small settlements of Russians in this country, for the sake of the skins of quadrupeds, which

---

* He lived during this winter in Queen Street, near Greenland Dock, Rotherhithe : he hath sailed, probably, by this time on the Greenland Fishery. With regard to his having been in North Latitude 81° 30′, in June, 1773, he can prove it by his Journal, if that evidence should be required.

† See the Narrative of eight sailors, who wintered in Greenland A. D. 1630, and who all returned in health to England the ensuing summer.—Churchill's Voyage, vol. iv, p. 811.

They did not see the sun from the 14th of October till the 3d of February. By the last day of January, however, they had day-light of eight hours. They wintered in North Latitude 77—4°.—Ibid.

are then more valuable than if the animal is taken in summer.

The next instance I shall mention of a navigator, who hath proceeded far Northward, is that of Captain Cheyne, who gave answers to certain queries drawn up by Mr. Dalrymple, F. R. S. in relation to the Polar Seas, and which were communicated last year to the Society.

Captain Cheyne states, in this paper, that he hath been as far as North Latitude 82°; but does not specify whether by *observation* or his *reckoning*, though from many other answers to the interrogatories proposed, it should seem that he speaks of the latitude by *obser-vation*. Unfortunately Captain Cheyne is at present on the Coast of Africa, so that farther information on this head cannot be now pro-cured from him.

Whilst the ships destined for the North Pole were preparing, a most ingenious and able Sea officer, Lieutenant John Cartwright, told me, that twelve years ago he had been informed of a very remarkable voyage made by Captain Mac-Callam as far nearly as 84° North Latitude.

This account Mr. Cartwright had received from a brother officer, Mr. James Watt, now a Master and Commander in the Royal Navy, who was on board Captain Mac-Callam's ship.

I thought it my duty to acquaint the Admiralty with this intelligence, who would have sent for Mr. Watt, but he was then employed on the coast of America.

On his return from thence, within the last month, Mr. Cartwright introduced a conversation with regard to Captain Mac-Callam's voyage, when Mr. Watt repeated all the circumstances which he had mentioned to him twelve years ago ; after which Mr. Cartwright, thinking that I should be glad to hear the particulars from Mr. Watt himself, was so good as to bring him to my chambers, when I received from him the following information.

In the year 1751 Mr. Watt, then not quite

seventeen years of age, went on board the
Campbeltown of Campbeltown, Captain Mac-
Callam, which ship was at that time employed
in the Greenland Fishery.

It seems, that, during the time the whales
are supposed to copulate, the crews of the
Greenland vessels commonly amuse themselves
on shore.

Captain Mac-Callam, however (who was a
very able and scientific seaman), thought that
a voyage to the North Pole would be more
interesting; and that, the season being a fine
one, he had a chance of penetrating far to the
Northward, as well as returning before the later
fishery took place. He accordingly proceeded
without the least obstruction to $83\frac{1}{2}°$, when
the sea was not only open to the Northward,
but they had not seen a speck of ice for the
last three degrees, and the weather at the
same time was temperate; in, short, Mr. Watt
hath never experienced a more pleasant navigation.

It need be scarcely observed, that the latitude

of $83\frac{1}{2}°$ was determined by observation, as the great object of the voyage was to reach the Pole; the Captain therefore, the Mate, and young Mr. Watt, determined the latitude from time to time, both by Davis and Hadley's quadrants: to this I may add, that their departure and return were from and to Hakluyt's Headland.

When they were advancing into these high Northern Latitudes, the Mate complained that the compass was not steady, on which Captain Mac-Callam desisted from his attempt, though with reluctance; knowing that if any accident happened, he should be blamed by his owners, who would be reminded certainly by the Mate of the protests he had made against the ship's proceeding farther Northward.

Several of the crew, however, were for prosecuting their discoveries, and Mr. Watt particularly remembers the chagrin which was expressed by a very intelligent seaman, whose name was John Kelly; Captain Mac-Callam, also, after his return from that voyage, hath frequently said, in the presence of Mr. Watt and others, that, if the Mate had not been faint-hearted, the ship possibly might have reached the Pole.

Both Captain Mac-Callam and the Mate are now dead, and it is rather doubtful whether the Ship's Journal can be procured.

It remains therefore to be considered what may be objected to the credibility of this very interesting account.

I have stated, that Mr. Watt was not, at the time this voyage took place, quite seventeen years of age; but I have also stated, that he observed himself (as well as the Master and Mate) from time to time. Is it therefore more extraordinary he should remember with accuracy, that, two and twenty years ago, he had been in North Latitude $83\frac{1}{2}°$, than that, at the same distance of time, he might recollect that he had been at a friend's house, which was situate eighty-three miles and a half from London? Or rather indeed is not his memory, with regard to this high latitude, much more to be depended upon, as the circumstance is so much more interesting, especially as Mr. Watt was even then of a scientific turn?

To this I may add, that it being his first voyage, and so remarkable a one, Mr. Watt now declares that he remembers more particulars relative to it, than perhaps in any other since that time : other sea officers have likewise told me, that the circumstances of their first voyages are most fresh in their memory, the reason for which is too obvious to be dwelt upon.

If Mr. Watt's recollection however is distrusted, this objection extends equally to Captain Mac-Callam's frequent declarations, that, if the apprehensions of the Mate had not prevented, he might possibly have reached the North Pole : and how could he have conceived this, unless he, had imagined himself to have been in a very high Northern Latitude?

But it may be possibly said, that this voyage took place above twenty years since, and that therefore, at such a distance of time, no one's memory can be relied upon.

It is true indeed, that Mac-Callam made this attempt in 1751; but Mr. Watt continued his services the following year in a Greenland Ship, and therefore, traversing nearly the same seas, must have renewed the recollection of what he had experienced in the preceding voyage, though he did not then proceed farther than North Latitude 80°.

This however brings it only to 1752; but I have already stated, that within these twelve years he mentioned all the particulars above related to his brother officer, Lieutenaut Cartwright.

Mr. Watt also frequently conversed with Captain Mac-Callam about this voyage after both of them had quitted the Greenland Ships; Mr. Watt rising regularly to be a Master and Commander in His Majesty's service, and Captain Mac-Callam becoming Purser of the Tweed Man of War.

It so happened, that in the year of the expedition against Bellisle, Mr. Watt, Captain Mac-Callam, and Mr. Walker (commonly called Commodore Walker, from his having commanded the Royal Family privateers in the late war), met together at Portsmouth, when they talked over the circumstances of this Greenland voyage, which Mr. Walker was interested in, by having been the principal owner of the Campbeltown.

Mr. Watt and Captain Mac-Callam met also eleven years ago in London, when they as usual conversed about the having reached so high a Northern Latitude.

I now come to my last proof, which I received from the late Dr. Campbell, the able continuator and reviser of Harris's Collection of Voyages.

In that very valuable compilation, Commodore Roggewein's circumnavigation makes a most material addition, some of the most interesting particulars of which were communicated by Dr. Dallie, who was a native of Holland*, and lived in Racquet Court, Fleet Street, about the year 1745, where he practised physic.

* He was a grandson of Dallie, who was author of a book, much esteemed by the Divines, entitled " *De Usu Patrum.*"

Dr. Campbell went to thank Dallie for the having furnished him with Roggewein's Voyage, when Dallie said, that he had been farther both to the Southward and to the Northward than perhaps any other person who ever existed.

He then explained himself as to the having been in high Southern Latitudes, by sailing in Roggewein's fleet*, and as to his having been far to the Northward, he gave the following account: —

Between fifty and sixty years ago it was usual to send a Dutch ship of war to superintend the Greenland Fishery, though it is not known whether this continues to be a regulation at present.

Dr. Dallie (then young) was on board the Dutch vessel employed on this service†; and during the interval between the two fisheries

* Roggewein reached South Latitude 62° 30'. — See Harris.

† Dr. Campbell does not recollect in what capacity he served; but, as he afterwards practised physic, he might probably have been the surgeon.

the Captain determined, like Mr. Mac-Callam,
to try whether he could not reach the Pole;
and accordingly penetrated (to the best of Dr.
Campbell's recollection) as far as North Latitude 88°, when the weather was warm, the sea
perfectly free from ice, and rolling like the Bay
of Biscay. Dallie now pressed the Captain to
proceed; but he answered, that he had already
gone too far by having neglected his station,
for which he should be blamed in Holland: on
which account, also, he would suffer no Journal
to be made, but returned as speedily as he could
to Spitzbergen.

There are undoubtedly two objections, which
may be made to this account of Dr. Dallie's,
which are, that it depends not only upon his
own memory, but that of Dr. Campbell, as no
Journal can be produced, for the reason which
I have before stated.

The conversation, however, between Dr.
Campbell and Dallie arose from the accidental
mention of Roggewein's Voyage to the Southward; and can it be supposed that Dallie

c

invented this circumstantial Narrative on the spot, without having actually been in a high Northern Latitude?

If this be admitted to have been improbable, was he not likely to have remembered with accuracy what he was so much interested about, as to have pressed the Dutch Captain to have proceeded to the Pole?

But it may be said, also, that we have not this account from Dallie himself, but at second hand from Dr. Campbell, at the distance of thirty-years from the conversation.

To this it may be answered, that Dr. Campbell's memory was most remarkably tenacious, as is well known to all those who had the pleasure of his acquaintance; and, as he hath written so ably for the promotion of geographical discoveries in all parts of the globe, such an account could not but make a strong impression upon him, especially as he received it just after the first edition of his compilation of voyages.

No one easily forgets what is highly interesting to him ; and, though I do not pretend
to have so good a memory as Dr. Campbell,
I have scarcely a doubt, but that, if I should
live thirty years longer, and retain my
faculties, I shall recollect with precision every
latitude which I have already stated in this
Paper.

What credit, however, is to be given to all
these narratives is entirely submitted to the
Society, as I have stated them most fully,
with every circumstance which may invalidate,
as well as support them ; and if I have endeavoured to corroborate them by the observations
which I have made, it is only because I believe
them.

It should seem upon the whole of the
inquiries on this point, that it is very uncertain when ships may proceed far to the
Northward of Spitzbergen ; and that it depends not only upon the season, but other
accidents, when the Polar Seas may be so

free from ice as to permit attempts to make discoveries *.

Possibly, therefore, if a king's officer was sent from year to year on board one of the Greenland ships, the lucky opportunity might be seized, and the Navy Board might pay for the use of the vessel, if it was taken from the Whale Fishery, in order to proceed as far as may be towards the North Pole.

* Captain Robinson hath informed me, that at the latter end of last April a Whitby Ship was in North Latitude 80°, without having been materially obstructed by the ice. Captain Marshall was also off Hakluyt's Headland so early as the 25th of April, without observing much ice.

DAINES BARRINGTON, F.R.S.

ADDITIONAL PROOFS,

&c. &c.

———◆———

Read at a Meeting of the Royal Society,

DEC^r 22, 1774.

════════════

AS I happen to have collected many additional facts since my Paper, containing Instances of Navigators who had reached high Northern Latitudes, was read before the Society in May last, I shall take the liberty to state them according to chronological order; together with some general reasons why it may be presumed, that the Polar Seas are, at least sometimes, navigable.

I think it my duty to do this, not only because I was the unworthy proposer of the Polar Voyage in 1773, which was recommended

by the Council of the Royal Society to the
Board of Admiralty; but because it would
not redound much to the credit of the Society,
if they planned a voyage to reach the North
Pole, if possible, when a perpetual barrier of
ice prevented any discoveries in the Spitzbergen
Seas to the Northward of $80\frac{1}{2}°$, which is not a
degree beyond the most common station of the
Greenland Fishers.

I must here however, repeat, that no one is
more entirely satisfied than myself of the great
abilities, perseverance, and intrepidity, with
which the officers, who were sent on this destination, attempted to prosecute their discoveries;
but I conceive from the arguments and facts
which will follow that they were stopped by a
most unfortunate barrier of ice (of great extent
indeed), but which was only temporary and not
perpetual.

If such a wall of ice hath been constantly
fixed in this latitude, and must continue to be
so, there is an end to all discoveries to be made
to the Northward of Spitzbergen; but if it is

only occasional, the attempt may be resumed in some more fortunate year *.

The point therefore being of so much importance to geography, I hope the Society will pardon me if I more fully enter into the subject than I did in my former Paper.

The English have long taken the lead in geographical discoveries. One of our ships of war is lately returned, after having penetrated into the Antarctic Circle; and is it not rather a reflection upon a scientific nation, that more is not known with regard to the circumpolar regions of our own hemisphere, than can be collected from maps made in the time of Charles I, especially when the run from the mouth of the Thames to the North Pole is not a longer one than from Falmouth to the Cape de Verde islands?

* Upon the first return of the king's ships from the Polar Voyage, this notion of a perpetual barrier of ice at North Latitude 80½ had prevailed so much, that some very distinguished philosophers of this country had shown thoughts of proceeding to the Pole over the ice, in such a wind boat as the Dutch have sometimes made use of.

Though I have the honour to be a Fellow of a Society instituted for the promotion of Natural Knowledge, the prejudices of an Englishman are so strong with me, that I cannot but wish the discoveries to be made in the Polar Seas may be achieved by my countrymen; but, if we are determined to abandon the enterprise, science is to be honoured from whatever quarter it may come, and it hath therefore given me great satisfaction to hear, that Mons. de Bougainville is soon to be sent on discoveries to the Northward*.

In the outset of my former Paper, I said I should not trouble the Society with any instances of navigators having reached high Northern Latitudes, which had appeared in print. During the course of this summer, however, I have happened to find three such accounts, which were never before alluded to, and which are extracted from books that are not

* I have since been informed, that this intended voyage was dropped, by the French minister for the marine department being changed.

commonly looked into, or at least often con-
sulted upon points of geography.

When the Royal Society was first instituted,
it was usual to send queries to any traveller who
happened to reside in England, after having
been in parts of the world which are not commonly frequented *.

In the year 1662-3, Mr, Oldenburg, the secretary of the Society, was ordered to register a
Paper, entitled, " Several Inquiries concerning
Greenland, answered by Mr. Grey, who had
visited those parts."

The 19th of these queries is the following : —

" How near any one hath been known to
approach the Pole ?

Answer. " I once met, upon the Coast of
Greenland, a Hollander, that swore he had been
but half a degree from the Pole, showing me
his Journal, which was also attested by his

* Richard Hakluyt rode two hundred miles to hear the
Narrative of Mr. Thomas Butt's Voyage, temp. Hen. VIII,
from England to Newfoundland.—Hakluyt, part iii, p. 131.

mate ; where they had seen no ice or land, but all water *."

After which Mr. Oldenburgh adds, as from himself, " This is incredible †."

It may not be improper, therefore, after mentioning this first instance of a navigator's having approached so near to the Pole, to dis-

---

* Mr. Boyle mentions a similar account, which he received from an old Greenland Master on the 5th of April, 1675. — See Boyle's Works, vol. ii, p. 397 to 399, folio. The whole of this Narrative is very circumstantial, and deserves to be stated at length. The title is Experiments and Observations made in December and January 1662.

† See Dr. Birch's History of the Royal Society, vol. i, p. 202. These queries are nineteen in number, to which the answers are very circumstantial. I had an opportunity of reading them over to three very intelligent masters of Greenland Ships, who confirmed every particular. One circumstance I think it right to take notice of, though it does not immediately relate to the point in discussion, which is, that there are coals in Spitzbergen, by which seven of Mr. Grey's crew were enabled to bear the severity of the winter, having been left behind by an accident. One of the Greenland Masters, to whom I read Mr. Grey's answers, confirmed this particular ; saying, that he had burnt himself Spitzbergen coals, and that they were very good.

cuss upon what reasons Mr. Oldenburgh might found this his very peremptory incredulity.

Was it because the fact is impossible upon the very stating it?

This puts me in mind of the disbelief which is generally shown to a passage in Pliny, even after the actual fact hath shown not only the possibility, but easy practicability of what is alluded to. Pliny informs us *, that Eudoxus, flying the vengeance of king Lathyrus, sailed from Arabia, and reached the Straits of Gibraltar: yet no one scarcely will believe this account of Eudoxus's navigation, notwithstanding this course is so often followed.

Was it because no Englishman had then been so far to the Northward?

It is very easy, however, to account why such attempts should rather be made by the Dutch than the English in the infancy of the Greenland Fishery.

The Southern parts of this country were

---

* Lib. ii, chap. lxvii.

discovered by Sir Hugh Willoughby, A. D.
1553; after which no English ships were sent
on that coast for nearly fifty years. In the
beginning of the last century, however, a com-
petition arose between the English and Dutch,
with regard to the Whale Fishery, and the
English drove the Dutch from most of the
harbours, under the right of first discoverers *,
in which they were supported by royal instructions; so that the Dutch were obliged to seek
for new stations, whereas the English were
commonly in possession of the Greenland Ports,
which they considered as their own †.

* It is also assigned, in the Supplement to Wood and
Marten's Voyages, p. 179, 8vo., 1694, as a reason why
the English never proceeded farther than 78° on the East
Coast of Spitzbergen, because the Dutch were commonly
superior on that side of the Island.

Robert Bacon, of Crowmers in Norfolk, was the first discoverer also of Iceland. — See the Itinerary of William of
Worcester, p. 311, 8vo., Cambridge, 1778.

† See Purchas, *passim.* Whilst these disputes continued,
the Dutch often sent ships of war to protect their Greenland Traders, which accounts for Dr. Dallie's sailing in such
a vessel to 88°, as I have stated in my former Paper.

Did Mr. Oldenburgh disbelieve the Dutch-man's relation, because ice is frequently met with to the Southward of North Latitude 80°?

Ice is commonly seen upon the great bank of Newfoundland, and the harbour of Louis-burgh is often covered with it, which is only in North Latitude 46°; yet Davis and Baffin have penetrated, under nearly the same me-ridians, beyond 70°.

I will now suppose the tables changed be-tween the two hemispheres of our globe, and that a Southern discoverer, meeting with ice upon the banks of Newfoundland, returns to his own hemisphere fully impressed with the impossibility of proceeding much to the North-ward of North Latitude 46°; would not his countrymen be deceived by the inferences which were drawn from what had been observed in the seas of the Northern hemisphere?

Bouvet, in 1738, sailed to 53° Southern Latitude, and in a meridian 5° to the West of the Cape of Good Hope, in which situation he fell in with floating ice; after which he did not proceed any farther. Our two ships of war, lately sent upon discoveries to the Southward, however, have been some minutes within the Antarctic Circle, upon a no very distant meridian from that in which Bouvet sailed.

Must the fact be disbelieved because all the ice in the Polar Seas comes from the Northward? But this is not so, as Mr. Grey informs us*, that the South East Wind brings the greatest quantity of ice to the coasts of Spitzbergen; which indeed is highly probable, as this wind blows from those parts of the Icy Sea into which the great rivers of Siberia and Tartary empty themselves†. My own poor conception, with regard to the floating ice in the Spitzbergen Seas, is, that these masses come

---

* Dr. Birch's History of the Royal Society.

† The ice is said to be never troublesome in the harbour of Newport (Rhode Island, North America); because no fresh water rivers empty themselves by this port; whereas the harbour of New York (though much to the Southward) is often obstructed by the ice, which floats down from Hudson's River.

almost entirely from the same quarter, as it is so difficult to freeze any large quantity of salt water. These pieces of ice, therefore, being once launched into the Icy Sea, are dispersed by winds, tides, and currents, in every direction, some of them being perhaps carried to very high Northern Latitudes, from which they are again wafted to the Southward.

But allowing, for an instant, that all the ice may come from the Northward, must not then an open sea be left in the higher Northern latitudes, from which these masses of ice are supposed to have floated?

Was it because the more one advances towards the Pole, vegetation invariably is diminished?—But this is not the fact.

Nova Zembla, situate only in North Latitude 76°, produces not even any sorts of grass*; so that the only quadrupeds which frequent it are foxes and bears, both of which are carnivorous. In the Northern parts of Spitzbergen,

---

* Purchas, vol. i, p. 479.

on the other hand, they have rein-deer, which
are often excessively fat; and Mr. Grey mentions three or four plants, which flower there
during the summer *.

Was it because no one had ever conceived
it possible to proceed so far as the Pole ✝ ?

Thorne, however, a merchant of Bristol,
had made snch a proposal in the reign of
Henry VIII; and I shall now also show, that
not only Mr. Oldenburgh's contemporaries continued to believe such a voyage to be feasible,
but many great names in science who lived after
him.

Wood sailed on the discovery of a North
East Passage to Japan in 1676; and, in the
publication of his voyage, he hath stated the
grounds upon which he conceived such a voyage

* Dr. Birch's History of the Royal Society, vol. i,
et. seq.

† A Map of the Northern Hemisphere, published at
Berlin (under the direction of the Academy of Sciences and
Belles Lettres), places a ship at the Pole, as having arrived
there according to the Dutch accounts.

to be practicable; the strongest of all which, perhaps, is the relation of Captain Goulden, with regard to a Dutch ship having reached North Latitude 89°. Though this account hath often been referred to, I do not recollect to have seen it stated with all the circumstances which seem to establish its veracity beyond contradiction : I shall therefore copy the very words of Wood *.

"Captain Goulden, who had made above thirty voyages to Greenland, did relate to his majesty, that, being at Greenland some twenty years before, he was in company with two Hollanders to the Eastward of Edge's Island†;

* Moxon's account of a Dutch ship having been two degrees beyond the Pole was also much relied upon by Wood, which hath never been printed at large, but in a now very scarce tract of Moxon's, and in the second volume of Harris's Voyage, p. 396. In confirmation of this very circumstantial and interesting narrative, I have only to add, that Moxon was hydrographer to Charles II, and hath published several scientific treatises. — See the Catalogue of the Bodleian Library.

† Edge's Island was discovered, A. D. 1616, by Captain

and that the whales not appearing on the shore, the two Hollanders were determined to go farther Northward, and in a fortnight's time returned, and gave it out that they had sailed into the Latitude 89°, and that they did not meet with any ice, but a free and open sea; and that there run a very hollow *grown** sea, like that of the Bay of Biscay. Mr. Goulden being not satisfied with the bare relation, they produced him four Journals out of the two ships, which testified the same, and that they all agreed within four minutes†."

Thomas Edge, who had made ten voyages to those seas. —See the Supplement to the North East Voyages, 8vo. London, 1694. Whyche's Island, so called from a gentleman of that name, was discovered in the following year. —Ibid.

* *Grown Sea* is the expression in the original. " Which is not practicable in these tempestuous high *grown* seas." — Dr. Halley, in his Journal, p. 45.

† Wood's Voyage, p. 145.—Wood's Voyage was published by Smith and Walford, Printers to the Royal Society in 1694, together with Sir John Narborough's, Marten's, and other Navigators. The book is dedicated to Pepys, Secretary to the Admiralty ; and he is complimented therein for having furnished the materials.

Having thus stated Wood's own words, it should seem, that they who deny the authenticity of the relation must contend, that the crews of both these Dutch ships entered into a deliberate scheme of imposing upon their brother Whale Fishers, and had drawn up four fictitious Journals accordingly, because so many are stated to have been produced out of the two ships to Captain Goulden, whilst each of them varied a few minutes in the latitude; whereas, if they had determined to deceive Captain Goulden and his crew, the Journals would probably have tallied exactly. I must beg leave also to make an additional observation on the account as stated by Wood, which is, that the Dutch ships only went to the Northward in search of whales, but did not give it out that they intended to make for the Pole, which if they had done, it might possibly have been an inducement to carry on the deception by forgeries and misrepresentations. To this it may likewise be added, that the Dutch are not commonly jokers.

I have already remarked, that **Wood** makes
this account one of the principal reasons for
his undertaking the North East Passage to
Japan. Wood therefore (Mr. Oldenburgh's
contemporary) was not a disbeliever before his
voyage of the possibility of reaching so high a
Northern Latitude, nor of any of the circumstances stated in this Narrative.

But Captain Wood is not a single instance
of such credulity, as, the very year before he
sailed on his Voyage, we find in the Philosophical Tsansactions for 1675 * the following
passage :—" For it is well known to all that
sail Northward, that most of the Northern
Coasts are frozen up many leagues, though in
the open sea it is not so, *No, nor under the Pole
itself*, unless by accident." In which passage,
the having reached the Pole is alluded to as
a known fact, and stated as such to the Royal
Society.

Wood indeed, after not being able to proceed

* No. 118.

farther than North Latitude 76°, discredits in the lump all the former instances of having reached high Northern Latitudes, in the following words :—

" So here the opinion of William Barentz was confuted, and all the Dutch relations*, which certainly are all forged and abusive pamphlets, as also the relations of our countrymen †."

In justice, however, to the memoirs of both English and Dutch Navigators, I cannot but take notice of these very peremptory and ill-founded reflections, made by Wood ; and which seem to be dictated merely by his disappointment, in not being able to effect his discovery.

Wood attempted to sail in a North East

---

* The Dutch made three voyages for the discovery of the North East Passage in three successive years, the third being in 1596, which last was by the encouragement of a private subscription only.— See Gerard de Veer, p. 13, folio, Amsterdam, 1609.

† Wood's Voyage, p. 181.

direction between Spitzbergen and Nova Zembla, but was obstructed by ice, so that he could
not proceed farther than the West Coast of
Nova Zembla, in North Latitude 76°. Thinking it, therefore, prudent to return, he at once
treats as fabulous, not only the ideas of that
most persevering seaman William Barentz, but
likewise all other accounts of ships having
reached high Northern Latitudes. Now that
the ice, which obstructed Wood in North Latitude 76°, was not a perpetual, but only occasional barrier, appears by the Russians having
not only discovered, but lived several years in
the island of Maloy Brun, which lies between
Spitzbergen and Nova Zembla, and extends
from North Latitude 77° 25′ to 78° 45′*. The
Dutch also sailed round the Northern Coast of

* See the English Translation of Professor Le Roy's
account of this Island, p. 85, 8vo., London, 1774, printed
for C. Heydinger. As also the Sieur de Vaugondy's *Essai
d'une Carte Polaire Arctique*, published in 1774, who re-
presents this island as extending from North Latitude
77° 20′ to 78° 30′, its longitude being 60° East from
Fero.

Nova Zembla, and wintered on the Eastern side in 1596 *.

As for Wood's treating all discoveries towards the Pole, from the Northern parts of Spitzbergen, as fabulous, he had not the least foundation, from what he had observed on his own voyage, for this unmerited aspersion upon their veracity; because, if Wood's barrier between Spitzbergen and Nova Zembla, in North Latitude 76°, had been perpetual, what hath this to do with the course of a ship sailing from the Northern parts of Spitzbergen upon a meridian towards the Pole?

I cannot however dismiss Wood's Voyage without making some farther remarks on his

* See the Map of the circumpolar regions, which accompanies Wood's Voyage. The Northern point of Nova Zembla, in this Map, is in 77° nearly. There were factions in Holland, with regard to the method of discovering the North East Passage. Barentz, instigated by Plancius the Geographer, was for making the trial to the North of Nova Zembla; the other two ships, which sailed on that expedition of discovery, were to attempt passing the Weygatz.— Recueil des Voyages au Nord, tom. iv. Linschoten's Preface.

concluding, that the obstructions which he met
with in North Latitude 76° were perpetual.

Almost every voyage to seas, in which
floating ice is commonly to be found, proves
the great difference between the quantities, as
well as size, of these impediments, to navigation, though in the same latitude and time of
the year.

Davis, in his two first voyages to discover
the North West Passage, could not penetrate
beyond 66°; but in his third voyage, in 1587,
he reached 72° 12′*.

In the year 1576, Sir Martin Frobisher
passed the Straits (since called from their first
discoverer) without any obstructions from ice;
in his two following voyages, however, he found
them in the same month, to use his own expression, "in a manner shut up with a long mure
of ice †."

In the year 1614, Baffin proceeded to 81°,

---

* See Hakluyt, and Purchas, vol. i, p. 84.

† Purchas, ibid.

and thought he saw land as far as 82°* to the North East of Spitzbergen, which is accordingly marked in one of Purchas's Maps. During this voyage he met near Cherry Island, situate only in 74° North Latitude, two banks of ice; the one, forty leagues in length, the other one hundred and twenty; which last would extend to twenty-five degrees of longitude in North Latitude, 76°, where Wood fixes his barrier.

It need therefore scarcely be observed, that such a floating wall of ice, one hundred and twenty leagues long, by being jammed in between land, or other banks of ice, might afford an appearance indeed of forming a perpetual barrier, when perhaps, within the next twenty-four hours, the wall of ice might entirely vanish.

Of the sudden assemblage of such an accumulation of ice, I shall now mention two, rather recent, instances.

---

* See also the Supplement to Wood and Marten's Voyages, in the 8vo. publication of 1694, in which point Purchas is stated to be in North Latitude 82°.

I have been very accurately informed, that
the late Colonel Murray happened to go, in
the month of May, from one of our Southern
Colonies to Louisburgh, when the harbour was
entirely open ; but, on rising in the morning, it
was completely filled with ice, so that a waggon
might have passed over it in any direction *.

I have also received the following account
from an officer in the Royal Navy, who was
not many years ago on the Newfoundland
station.

In the middle of June, the whole Straits of
Bellisle were covered in the same manner with
the harbour of Louisburgh, and for three weeks

---

* On the 19th of December, 1759, the Potowmack,
in a part where it was two miles broad, and nearly in
North Latitude of only 38°, was frozen entirely over
in one night, when the preceding day had been very
mild and temperate. — Burnaby's Travels through North
America, p. 59.

Camden, in his Annals of Elizabeth, asserts, that Davis
reached 83°, where the Straits, called after him, were
narrowed to forty leagues. — See Camden, anno 1585.
We have not since been able to proceed so far to the
Northward.

together a carriage might have passed from one shore to the other; but during a single night the ice had almost entirely disappeared. Such is the sudden accumulation of ice, in latitudes twenty-four and thirty degrees to the Southward of Wood's situation.

Linschoten asserts, that being in the Straits of Weygate the last day of July, he was told by the Samoieds on that coast, that in ten or twelve days afterwards the ice in the Straits would be all gone, though they were then quite blocked up with it. When he repassed these Straits afterwards, on the 13th of August, he found not the least vestige of it, so quickly do these huge masses dissolve after they once begin to thaw*.

On the other hand, Callander admits, that by accumulation of floating ice places are now inaccessible which were not formerly so, and instances the Eastern Coast of Greenland, as also Frobisher's Straits†. Kergulen, in his account

---

* Callander's Preface, p. 38   † Ibid.

of Iceland, likewise mentions, that the sea between Iceland and Greenland was entirely closed
during the whole summer of 1766.

I shall now endeavour to show, that
Dr. Halley was no more incredulous with regard to the possibility of reaching high Northern
Latitudes, than Captain Wood was before the
ill success of his voyage on discovery.

Mr. Miller, in his Gardener's Dictionary,
hath the following passage, under the article
THERMOMETER :—

" Mr. Patrick has fixed his thermometer to
a scale of 90°, which are numbered from the
top downwards, and also a moveable index to
it. The design of this is to show, how the heat
and cold is changed from the time it was last
looked upon, according to the different degrees
of heat and cold in all latitudes. As by the
trial of two thermometers, which have *been
regulated abroad;* the one by Dr. Halley, in his
late Southern Voyage; and the other by Captain Johnson, in his voyage to Greenland; the
first hath a heat under the equinoctial line,

and the other a degree of cold in 88° of North
Latitude."

I have taken some pains to find out a more
full account of this voyage of Captain Johnson's; but have only met with the following
confirmation of it perhaps :—

" I have been assured, *by persons of credit*,
that an English Captain, whose name was
Monson, instead of seeking a passage to China
between the Northern countries, had directed
his course to the Pole, and had approached it
within two degrees, where there was an open
sea without any ice *."

As the Captain Monson mentioned in this
passage reached exactly the same degree of
latitude with Captain Johnson, I should rather
think, that this is the same voyage; especially,
as it is well known, that the French writers
seldom trouble themselves about the orthogra-
phy of foreign names.

If this, however, should not be the case, it

* See M. de Buffon's Natural History, vol. i, p. 215, 4to.

must be admitted to be an additional instance of a ship's having reached North Latitude 88°, as well as Mons. de Buffon's giving credit to such relation*.

Having therefore not been able to pick up any other circumstances in relation to Captain Johnson's Voyage, I shall now state what seems to be fairly deducible from the passage, which I have copied from Miller's Gardener's Dictionary.

Dr. Halley made his voyage to the Southward in 1700; on the return from which, he probably employed Patrick, as the most eminent maker of weather glasses†, to graduate a thermometer

* To this list of credulous persons (as perhaps they may be considered by some), I shall beg leave to add the names of Maclaurin and Dr. Campbell. The former of these was so persuaded of the seas being open quite to the Pole, that he hath not only advised this method of prosecuting discoveries, but, as I have been told, was desirous of going the voyage himself.

† I have been informed, that his shop was in the Old Bailey, and that he died about fifty years ago. Patrick was a great ringer, and some of the most celebrated peals were

according to the heat he had experienced under the equator. It was very natural therefore, when such a point of heat was to be marked upon the instrument, to make the scale either for high Southern or Northern Latitudes.

It should seem, then, that Dr. Halley had procured Captain Johnson (who was Master of a Greenland Ship) to carry a thermometer on his voyage to Spitzbergen, and that he fortunately was able to reach so high a degree of latitude as 88°.

If the thermometer had been calculated only for imaginary degrees of heat and cold, it would have been marked for the Equator and the Pole; whereas it was only regulated for 88° of North Latitude, which Captain Johnson therefore had as clearly reached, as Dr. Halley had the Equator.

At all events, Patrick's Thermometer must have been made under Dr. Halley's inspection;

invented by him more than fifty years ago. He styled himself, in his advertisements, Torricellian Operator. — Sir John Hawkins's History of Music, vol. iv, p. 154.

and would he have permitted it to be marked
for 88° of North Latitude, according to Captain
Johnson's Voyage, if he had disbelieved his
Narrative?

My third and last instance, from any printed
authority, but in a book which is not commonly to be met with, is that of Captain Alex-
ander Cluny, as by a Map engraved under
his direction, the very spot is marked to the
Westward of Spitzbergen, and in somewhat
more than 82° of North Latitude, where he saw
neither land nor ice *.

Before I proceed, however, to state several
other instances of reaching high Northern Latitudes which have never appeared in print, and
which I have collected since my last Paper on this
head, I must beg the indulgence of the Society,
whilst I lay before them some additional rea-

---

* See the American Traveller, 4to. London, 1769; as,
also, the Sieur de Vaugondy's *Essai d'une Carte Polaire
Arctique,* published in 1774; in which, however, he lays
down this spot from Cluny's Map in little more than 81°,
whereas it is fully in 82°. The longitude of this spot is 30°
East from Fero.

sons why the Polar Seas may be conceived to be navigable *.

Speculative geographers have supposed, that there should be nearly the same quantity of land and sea in both hemispheres in order to preserve the equilibrium of the globe. It is possible, indeed, that this may be accounted for by the Antarctic Seas being more shallow than those near the North Pole; as we do not know this, however, by the actual soundings, but are informed by Captain Furneaux, that there is no land even as far as the Antarctic Circle, upon the meridian in which

* I have received a letter from the Rev. Mr. Tooke, Chaplain to the Factory at St. Petersburgh, dated December 30, 1774, which he concludes in the following manner:— "I have a fact or two to communicate, which seem to indicate, if not to a certainty, yet at least to a degree of probability, that the sea is open to the Pole the year throughout; but my paper will not hold them." From the accuracy with which several other interesting particulars are stated in this letter, I have great reason to regret, that I have not an opportunity of laying the facts alluded to before the Public, with all their circumstances, as I suppose that Mr. Tooke's information came from Archangel Seamen.

E

he sailed, as also that no land was observed during the course of his circumnavigation in 55° South Latitude at a medium, it seems necessary, as the quantity of land so greatly preponderates in the Northern hemisphere, that from North Latitude $80\frac{1}{2}°$ to the Pole itself must be chiefly, if not entirely, sea *.

Let us now consider, whether such a sea is probably, at all times, in a state of congelation.

I do not know, whether it hath been settled by thermometrical observations, that there is any material difference between the heat under the Equator, and that which is experienced within the Tropics; most travellers complain indefinitely of its excess in such latitudes.

As this point, therefore, seems not to have been settled by the thermometer, let us have recourse to what is found to be the freezing point upon mountains, situate almost under the Equator, and compare it with the same

* It is now known that Captain Cook also found very little land during his persevering attempts to the Southward.

height on the Peak of Teneriffe, which, being in
North Latitude 28°, is five degrees to the Northward of the tropical limits.

The French Academicians suppose, that the
freezing point, at which all vegetation ceases,
and ice takes place, commences, on Cotopaxi, at
1411 toises above the level of the sea; or, by
our measure, at the height of about a mile and
three quarters *.

Mr. Edens, on the other hand, hath given
us a very particular account of what he observed
in going to the top of Teneriffe †; and so far
from seeing snow or ice (except in a cave) his
coat was covered, during the night, with dew, at
the very summit; which, according to Dr. He-

* Cotopaxi is the highest mountain of the Andes, at
least in the neighbourhood of Quito. The plain of Cara-
buca, from which it rises, is 1023 toises above the level of
the sea, and the height of the mountain above this plain is
1268 toises, making together 2291 toises. If 880 toises
therefore are deducted from 2291, 1411 toises becomes the
height of the freezing point upon this mountain. — See
Ulloa's Account of South America.

† Philosophical Transactions Abridged, vol. v, p. 147;
Sprat's History of the Royal Society.

berden's computation, is 15,396 feet high, or
wants but 148 yards of three miles *.

Now, as it is thus settled, that the Peak of
Teneriffe is nearly three miles high, which exceeds by more than a mile the height of the
freezing point on Cotopaxi, situate under the
Equator, it should seem that there is no material
difference between the heat under the Equator
and within the Tropics ; for if it is urged, that
Teneriffe is more surrounded with sea than
Cotopaxi, it must on the other hand be recol-
lected, that this mountain is situate 5° to the
Northward of the Tropic, at the same time that
the summit exceeds the freezing point on Cotopaxi by more than a mile; both which circumstances should render it colder than the freezing
point on Cotopaxi.

The inference to be drawn from this com-
parison seems to be, that as the heat varies so
little between the Equator and the tropical

* See Hawkesworth's Voyages, vol. ii, p. 12. Goats also
reach the very summit, which must be in search of food, as
they do not bear cold well.

limits, it may differ as little between the Arctic
Circle and the Pole.

Nothing hath been supposed to show more
strongly the wisdom of a beneficent Creator,
than that every part of this globe should (taking
the year throughout) have an equal proportion
of the sun's light.

It is admitted, that the equatorial parts have
rather too much heat for the comforts of the inhabitants, and those within the Polar Circles too
little; but, as we know that the tropical limits
are peopled, it should seem that the two Polar
Circles are equally destined for the same purpose; or if not for the benefit of man, at least
for the sustenance of certain animals.

The largest of these, in the whole scale of
Creation, is the whale; which, though a fish,
cannot live long under water, without occasionally raising its head into another element, for
the purpose of respiration *: most other fish

* " Sometimes the ice is *fixed*, when there are but few
whales seen, for underneath the ice they cannot breathe."—
Marten's Voyage to Spitzbergen.

The whales, likewise, are supposed to come from the North;
but how can this be, if there is an incrusted sea over them?

also occasionally approach the surface of the
water.

If the ice therefore extends from North Latitude 80½° to the Pole, all the intermediate space
is denied to the Spitzbergen whales, as well
perhaps as to other fish. And is that glorious
luminary, the sun, to shine in vain for half
the year upon ten degrees of latitude round
each of the Poles, without contributing either
to animal life or vegetation? for neither can
take place upon this dreary expance of ice.

If this tract of sea also is thus rendered improper for the support of whales, these enormous fish, which require so much room, will
be confined to two or three degrees of latitude
in the neighbourhood of Spitzbergen; for all
the Greenland Masters agree, that the best
fishing stations are from 79° to 80°, and that
they do not often catch them to the Southward.

I will now ask, if the sea is congealed from
North Latitude 80½° quite to the Pole, when
did it thus begin to freeze, as it is well known,
that a large quantity of sea water is not easily

forced to assume the form of ice * ? Can it be
contended, that ten degrees of the globe round
each Pole were covered with frozen sea at the
original creation † ? And if this is not insisted

* " There are three kinds of ice in the Northern Seas.
The first is like melted snow, which is become partly har-
dened, is more easily broken into pieces, less transparent,
is seldom more than six inches thick, and, when dissolved,
is found to be intermixed with salt. This first sort of ice is
the only one which is ever formed from sea water.

" If a certain quantity of water, which contains as much
salt as sea water, is exposed to the greatest degree of cold,
it never becomes firm and pure ice, but resembles tallow or
suet, whilst it preserves the taste of salt, so that the *sweet*
transparent ice can never be formed in the sea. If the ice
of the sea itself, therefore, confined in a small vessel without any motion, cannot thus become true ice, much less
can it do so in a deep and agitated ocean." The author
hence infers, that all. the floating ice in the Polar Seas
comes from the Tartarian Rivers and Greenland, as I have
before contended. — See a Dissertation of Michel Lomo-
nosof, translated from the Swedish Transactions of 1752.
Collection Académique, tom. xi, p. 5, *et seq.,* 4to, Paris, 1772.
The Dissertation is entitled, " *De l'Origine des Monts de
Glace, dans la Mer du Nord.*"

† If there had been a fixed barrier of ice from the time
of the creation, extending from $80\frac{1}{2}°$ to the North Pole, the
height of such ice must have been excessive, by the accu-

upon, can it be supposed, that, when the surface of the Polar Ocean first ceased to be liquid it could have afterwards resisted the effects of winds, currents, and tides?

I beg leave also to rely much upon the necessity of the ice's yielding to the constant reciprocation of the latter; because no sea was ever known to be frozen but the Black Sea, and some small parts of the Baltic*, neither of which have any tides, at the same time that the waters of both contain much less salt than those of other seas, from the great influx of many fresh water rivers. For this last reason, it may likewise be presumed, that the circumpolar seas are very salt, because there is probably no such influx beyond North Latitude 80°, Spitzbergen itself having no rivers.

Having thus given some general reasons,

---

mulation of frozen snow from winter to winter. Marten therefore observes, that the ice mountains in Spitzbergen are constantly increasing by the snow and rain which falls freezing, and which seldom melts at the top.—P. 43.

* To these perhaps may be added the White Sea.

why the sea should not be supposed to be frozen in the ten highest degrees of latitude, I shall now proceed to lay before the Society several instances, which I have lately collected, and which prove that it is not so covered with ice considerably to the North of $80\frac{1}{2}°$.

I shall, however, previously make two obser vations ; the first of which is, that every instance of exceeding North Latitude $80\frac{1}{2}°$, as much proves that there is no perpetual barrier of ice in that latitude, as if the navigator hath reached the Pole. The second is, that as four experienced Greenland Masters have concurred in informing me, that they can see what is called the *blink of the ice** for a degree before them, they never can be off Hakluyt's

* This is described to be an arch formed upon the clouds by reflection from the *packed ice*. Where the ice is *fixed* upon the sea, you see a snow white brightness in the skies, as if the sun shined, for the snow is reflected by the air just as a fire by night is, but at a distance you see the air blue or blackish. Where there are many small ice fields, which are as meadows for the seals, you see no lustre or brightness of the skies.—Marten's Voyage to Spitzbergen.

Headland, which is situate in 79° 50', without observing this effect of the ice upon the sky, if there was a perpetual barrier at $80\frac{1}{2}°$, which is not much more than half a degree from them, when in that situation. Now Hakluyt's Headland is what they so perpetually take their departure from, that it hath obtained the name of *The Headland* by way of pre-eminence.

This mountain also is so high, that it can be distinguished at the distance of a degree: in such instances, therefore, which I shall produce, that do not settle the latitude by observation, whenever the reckoning depends upon the approach or departure from this Headland, the account receives the additional check of the mountain's being increased or diminished gradually to the eye of the observer.

My second previous remark shall be, with regard to all instances of reaching high Northern Latitudes, for which the authority of the Ship's Journal may be required, that it is almost impossible to procure this sort of evidence, except the voyages have been recent ; not only for the reasons I have given in my former Paper, but because I find, that if the Ship's Journal is not wanted by the owners in a year or two (which seldom happens) it is afterwards considered as waste paper.

Without the least impeachment also of the knowledge in navigation of the Greenland Masters, when they are in the actual pursuit of fish, they do not trouble themselves about their longitude or latitude ; they are not bound by their instructions to sail to any particular point, and their only object is to catch as many whales as possible ; the ship's situation therefore, at such time, becomes a matter of perfect indifference. It will appear, however, that they not only keep their reckonings, but observe, when they are not thus employed in fishing.

Having made these previous remarks, I shall now proceed to lay before the Society such instances of navigators having penetrated beyond $80\frac{1}{2}°$ as I have happened to procure since the reading of my former Paper on this subject, in May last.

James Hutton (then belonging to the ship London, Captain Guy) was, thirty years ago, in North Latitude 81½°, as both the Captain and Mate informed him; but he did not observe himself. A very intelligent sea officer was so good as to take from him this account, together with the following particulars, which perhaps may be interesting to Greenland Navigators.

Hutton hath been employed in the Whale Fishery nearly these forty years, during which he hath been several times at the Seven Islands, and the Waygat Straits. In some of these voyages the sea hath been perfectly clear from ice, and at other times it hath set in so rapidly towards the Waygat*, as to oblige the vessels which happened to be thereabouts to force all sail possible, to escape being inclosed.

* The Weighgatt is so called from the wind which blows through this Strait (*weihen*, to blow), because a strong South West Wind blows out of it. Another name for it is *Hindelopen.*—See Marten's Voyage, p. 27.

This hardy old tar likewise supposes, that he hath been farther up the Waygat than perhaps any person now living; for he was once in a ship which attempted to pass through it, nor did the master desist, till they shoaled the water to three fathoms, when the sea was so clear, that they could distinguish the bottom from the deck.

Mr. John Phillips, now master of the Exeter, but then Mate of the Loyal Club, in the year 1752, reached North Latitude 81° and several minutes by observation, which circumstance was confirmed by another person on board the Exeter last summer, on her return from the Greenland Fishery. Captain Phillips added, that it was *very common* to fish in such latitudes.

Mr. George Ware, now living at Erith in Kent, served as chief Mate in the year 1754, on board the Sea Nymph, Captain James Wilson, when, at the latter end of June, they sailed through floating ice from 74° to 81°; but having then proceeded beyond the ice they pursued the whales to 82° 15', which latitude was determined by Mr. Ware's own observation.

As the sea was now perfectly clear, as far as he could distinguish with his best glasses, both Mr. Ware and Captain Wilson had a strong inclination to push farther towards the Pole; but the common sailors hearing of such their intention, remonstrated, that if they should be able to proceed so far, the ship would fall into pieces, as the Pole would draw all the iron work out of her.

On this Captain Wilson and Mr. Ware desisted, as the crew had these very singular apprehensions; especially as they had no whales in sight to the Northward, which alone would justify the attempt to their owners*. It need scarcely be observed, however, that the notion which prevailed among the crew shows, that the common seamen on board the Greenland

---

* This circumstance of not seeing any whales in that direction accounts for Captain Guy's desisting, in the following instance, from sailing to the Northward, as also in many others which I shall have occasion to state.

Ships conceive, that the sea is open to the Pole; they would otherwise have objected on account of the ice being supposed to increase. It should seem also, that the practicability of reaching thé Pole is a point which they often discuss among themselves.

In *this same year and month,* Mr. John Adams (who now is master of a flourishing academy at Waltham Abbey, in Essex) was on board the Unicorn, Captain Guy, when they anchored in Magdalena Bay*, on the Western Coast of Spitzbergen and North Latitude 79° 35'.

They continued in this bay for three or four days, and then stood to the Southward, when the wind freshening from that quarter, but the weather foggy, they proceeded with an easy sail for four days, expecting to meet with fields of ice, to which they might make fast; but they did not encounter so much as a piece that floated. On the fifth day the wind veered to

* The Greenland Masters most commonly call this Bay Mac-Helena.

the Westward, the weather cleared up, and Mr. Adams had a good observation (the Sun above the Pole*) by which he found himself three degrees to the Northward of Hakluyt's Headland, or in North Latitude 83°.

Captain Guy now declared, that he had never been so far to the Northward before, and crawled up to the maintopmast head, accompanied by the chief mate, whilst the second mate together with Mr. Adams went to the foretopmast head, from whence they saw a sea as free from ice as any part of the Atlantic Ocean, and it was the joint opinion of them all, that they might have reached the North Pole.

The ship then stood to the Southward, and twelve hours afterwards Mr. Adams had a second good observation (the Sun beneath the Pole) when their latitude was 82° 3'. In both these observations Mr. Adams made an allowance of 5' for the refraction, which, he says, was his captain's rule, who was now on his

* The old navigators to these parts call this a *South Sun.*

fifty-ninth or sixtieth voyage to the Greenland Seas.

In the year 1756, Mr. James Montgomery, now a merchant in Prescot Street, Goodman's Fields, but then master of the Providence, followed the whales during the month of June till he reached North Latitude 83°, by observation. Another Greenland Master informs me, that he remembers well the ice packed much to the Westward, but that the sea was open to the Northward during that summer.

In 1762, David Boyd, then mate of the brig Betsey, was driven by a gale of wind from 79° to 82°, odd minutes, by observation; during all which time he was beset in ice. A Greenland Master has likewise told me, that he recollects many other ships were driven to the North East from their fishing stations during that season.

Mr. Jonathan Wheatley, now master of a Greenland Ship, was in 1766 off Hakluyt's Headland*, whence, not meeting with success,

* He was then on board a ship called the Grampus.

F

he sailed North West to 81½, in which latitude he could see no ice in any direction whatsoever from the mast head, although there was a very heavy sea from the North East.

Mr. Wheatley also informs me, that whilst he was off the Coast of Greenland, three Dutch Captains told him, that a ship of their nation had been in 89°, and they all supposed, that the sea in such a latitude might be as free from ice as where they were fishing. This account probably alludes to the Dutch man of war, on board of which Dr. Dallie happened to be, the circumstances of which voyage I have stated in my former Paper.

This same Captain is so thoroughly persuaded of being able to approach the Pole, that he will attempt it whenever an opportunity offers of doing it, without prejudice to his owners. On such a voyage of discovery, he would not wish a larger vessel than one of ninety tons *,

* Clipperton reached China in a bark not much exceeding ten tons, as did also Funnell, in another such vessel.—Callander, vol. iii, p. 223.

nor more than ten hands : I find, indeed, that this is the size of the ship in which most of the early navigators attempted to proceed far to the Northward.

In 1769, Mr. John Thew, now Master of a Greenland Ship called the Rising Sun, was in North Latitude 82°, and one hundred leagues to the West of Hakluyt's Headland. The circumstances by which he supposed himself to have been in this situation were stated to me in the presence of a very able sea officer, who told me afterwards, that he was perfectly satisfied with the accuracy of his account.

Captain John Clarke of the Sea Horse, at the latter end of June, 1773, sailed from the Headland North North East to $81\frac{1}{2}°$, which he computed by his run from the Headland in eighteen hours, having lost sight of it. At this time there was an open sea to the Northward, and such a swell from the North East, that the ship would not stay, being under her double reefed topsails, whilst the wind blew fresh.

During this run from the Headland, Mr. Clarke fell in with Captain Robinson in 81° 20′, whom I mentioned in my former Paper as having reached $81\frac{1}{2}$ in the same month and year, by a very accurate observation.

This same Captain Robinson, on the 28th of June last, passed by Hakluyt's Headland, lying off and on for several days, during which he was sometimes a degree to the Northward of it, and, till the 20th of July following, there was no obstruction to his proceeding Northward ; to which, however, he had no inducement, as he caught two large whales in this latitude*.

Captain John Reed of the Rockingham, also in July last, pursued some whales fifteen leagues to the Northward of the Headland, and confirms Captain Robinson's last account, by

* The Second Part of Marten's voyage (who received certain queries from the Royal Society) begins almost by saying, " We sailed to the 81st degree, and no ship ventured farther that year," *viz.* 1671.

saying he could then see no ice from his mast head.

Captain Reed was brought up in the Greenland Fishery, and remembers well, that whilst on board his father's ship, the Thistle, the Mate told him, that they had reached 81° 42', when there was indeed a good deal of ice, but full room to sail in any direction.

Mr. Reed likewise hath informed me, that about fifteen years ago, a Dutch Captain (whose name was Hans Derrick) told him, whilst they were together in the Greenland Seas, that he had been in North Latitude 86°, when there were only some small pieces of floating ice to be seen. Hans Derrick moreover added, that there were then five other ships in company, which took one with another eighteen small whales.

I have great reason to expect several other instances of the same kind, in a short time, from the different ports of this kingdom where there is any considerable Greenland Trade: I shall not, however, trouble the Society with them, till I know whether they would wish any farther information on this head.

I shall now recapitulate the different latitudes which have been reached by the several navigators whose names I have mentioned in this and my former Paper. I shall also take credit for nearly a degree to the Northward of their several situations, because the *blink or glare* of the *packed ice* is to be distinguished at this distance, when the weather is tolerably fair.

Captain John Reed................................ 80° 45′.
Captain Thomas Robinson (for three weeks
    together).. 81°.
Captain John Phillips............................. 81° odd mi.
James Hutton, Jonathan Wheatley, Thomas
    Robinson, John Clarke (four instances)...... 81° 30′.
Captains Cheyne and Thew (two instances.... 82°.
Cluny and David Boyd (two instances)......... 82° odd mi.
Mr. George Ware.................................. 82° 15′.
Mr. John Adams and Mr. James Montgomery
    (two instances)...................................... 83°.
Mr. James Watt, Lieutenant in the Royal
    Navy.. 83° 30′.

Five ships in company with Hans Derrick...... 86°.

Captain Johnson and Dr. Dallie (two instances; to which, perhaps, may be added
Captain Monson, as a third)..................... 88°.

Relation of the two Dutch Masters to Captain
Goulden *... 89°.

Dutch relation to Mr. Grey....................... 89 30'.

DAINES BARRINGTON, F.R.S.

* This instance, however, hath before been relied upon,
though never, perhaps, circumstantially stated but by
Captain Wood.

POSTSCRIPT.

———◆———

January 8, 1775.

HAVING procured the three following instances before the reading of my Paper was finished, it may not be improper to add them in a Post-script.

In Harris's voyages* is the following pas-sage:—"By the Dutch Journals they get into North Latitude 88° 56′, and the sea open."

I have, within these few days, asked Dr. Campbell, the very able compiler of these voyages, upon what authority he inserted this account? who informs me, that he received it from Holland about thirty years ago, as being an extract from the Journals produced to the

---

* Vol. ii, page 453.

States General in 1665, on the application for a
discovery of the North East Passage to Japan,
which was frustrated by the Dutch East-India
Company.

In the *Journal des Sçavans*, for the month
of October 1774*, is likewise the following
paragraph :—

" To these instances, produced by Mr. Barrington" (of navigators having reached high
Northern Latitudes), " our countrymen" (*viz.*
the Dutch) " could add many others. An able
officer in the English service hath in his cus-
tody the Journals of a Greenland Ship, wherein
he hath remarked, that in the month of May
he had penetrated as far as 82° 20′, when the
sea was open."

My third and last instance is that of Captain Bateson, who sailed in 1773, from Liverpool, in a ship called the Whale, on the
Greenland Fishery, and who, on June 14,
reached North Latitude 82° 15′, computed by

* Part ii, page 503.

his run back to Hakluyt's Headland *. As this happened so recently, Captain Bateson (as well as many of the other Masters, whose accounts I have before mentioned) hath his Journal to produce, if it should be required.

This seems to be the strongest confirmation of both Captain Robinson and Captain Clarke's having been, during this same year and month, in $81\frac{1}{2}°$; as also of their having met each other in 81° 20', according to what I have already stated.

I must not lose this same opportunity of laying before the Society the information, which I have just now received from M. de Buffon, in relation to what I have cited from his Natural History of Captain Monson's having reached North Latitude 88°, " *as he was told by persons of credit.*"

Upon my taking the liberty to inquire *who*

---

* His inducement to proceed so far North was the pursuit of whales. I have shown the extracts from Captain Bateson's Journal to a very able sea officer, who is perfectly satisfied with the accuracy of it.

those persons of credit were? M. de Buffon re-
fers me to Dr. Nathan Hickman, who, in 1730,
travelled as one of Dr. Ratcliff's fellows * ; and
who supposed, that Captain Monson's Journal
might have been at that time procured in
England. M. de Buffon also recollects, that a
Dutchman was then present, and confirmed the
account.

* He was also a fellow of the Royal Society in 1730,

ADDITIONAL PAPERS

FROM

HULL.

—————————

WHILST I was waiting in expectation of several additional instances of Dutch ships, which had been in high Northern Latitudes, I received the following answers to certain Queries relative to the Greenland Seas from a very eminent Merchant of Hull, and which he is so obliging as to permit me to lay before the Public.

D. B————.

March 31, 1775.

I.

FROM CAPTAIN JOHN HALL,

OF

THE KING OF PRUSSIA.

First Query. How near hath any ship approached the Pole?

Answer. I have known ships go into the latitude of 84° North, and did not hear of any difficulty they met with; but it is not often that the ice will permit them to go so far North.

N. B. On inquiring of Captain Hall what ships he had known proceed so far? He replied, they were some Dutch ships he heard had done so, but knew no particulars.

Second Q. When are the Polar Seas most free from ice?

A. The seas are most incumbered with ice from about the 1st of September to the 1st of

June following; and, in consequence, between the 1st of June and September, the ice lieth farthest from Spitzbergen. And I know no other precaution to be taken, respecting the Pole, than that they must watch the opportunity when the ice lieth farthest from the land.

Third Q. How far to the Southward have you first seen ice?

A. In the space of twenty years, I have twice known that we met with the ice in the latitude of 74° 30′ North, and could not find a passage to the Northward till the month of July, and then got into the latitude of 78° with much difficulty, in running through the openings of great bodies of ice; and some years we find a passage to the latitude 79 and 80° North, without much difficulty from the ice. Some years I have known ships go round the North part of Spitzbergen, and so come out between Nova Zembla and the South part of Spitzbergen; but this passage is seldom to be found free from ice.

Fourth Q. From what quarter is the wind coldest whilst off Spitzbergen?

A. Northerly and East North East Winds are most frosty; but snow and frost we have very common with all winds, except during part of June, July, and August. If the winds be Southerly the weather is milder, but subject to snow, sleet, and thick weather. The winds, currents, and the ice are very variable.

The opinion of the old seamen is, that we may proceed farther North than ever has been yet attempted; but this must be done with caution. An opportunity is to be watched for in those seas. The most likely time for such discoveries to be made is in the months of July and August, when the ice is most commonly farthest from the land; but some years not to be found open at all from the land. And when it is open, they must observe the ice to lay a long way from the North part of Spitzbergen; for I have known ships that made attempts to go to the Northward, and before they returned back, the ice set in with the land, so that they have been obliged to leave the ships to the East of Spitzbergen.

N.B. The ice always sets in with the land the back of the year.

II.

FROM CAPTAIN HUMPHREY FORD,

OF

THE MANCHESTER.

First. I was once as high as the latitude 81° 30′ North, in the ship Dolphin of Newcastle, in the year 1759 or 60, and have been several times since as high as the latitude 81° in the ships Annabella and Manchester, in which latitude I never met with any uncommon circumstances, but such as I have met with in the latitudes 75, 76, 77, 78, and 79°; if to the Westward, I was commonly incumbered with large quantities of ice.

Second. I suppose that the Greenland Seas are most incumbered with ice in the months of

G

December, January, February, and March; for
in the latter part of April and the first of May
the ice generally begins to separate and open;
and in the months of June and July we generally find the Greenland Seas most clear of ice.

Third. The only precaution to be taken, in
order to proceed towards the Pole, is to fit out
two strong ships, that are handy and sail fast,
well equipped, and secured in the manner of
those that are generally sent to Greenland on the
Whale Fishery. Such ships should be manned
with about forty able seamen in each, and
victualled for eighteen months or two years,
and be entirely under the command of some
expert, able, and experienced seaman, who
has frequented those seas for some time past.
They should sail from England about the middle of April, in order to be in with the edge of
the ice about the 10th of May, when it begins
to separate and open.

Fourth. There is not the least reason to

suppose, that the seas to the West, North West, and North of Spitzbergen are covered with permanent and perpetual ice, so as never to be opened by the operation of the winds ; for daily experience shows us, that a Northerly Wind, when of any long duration, opens and separates the ice, so as to admit the ships going amongst it in sundry places to a very high latitude, if attempted.

N.B. I never was to the Eastward of Spitzbergen ; but am of opinion, that the ice is much the same there as to the North and North West of Spitzbergen.

I generally find, that Northerly winds bring frost and snow ; on the contrary, Southerly Winds bring mild weather and rain ; but none of those winds appear to be periodical, except close in with the land called Fair Foreland, where I generally find the winds in the months of June and July to blow mostly from South South West, and very often excessive strong.

It is my opinion, by observing the above, that in some years ships might sail very nigh the Pole, if not, the impracticability must arise from the large quantity of ice that lies in those seas.

III.

FROM CAPTAIN RALPH DALE,

OF

THE ANN AND ELIZABETH.

I am willing to give you my opinion, in regard to the Queries received of you, so far as my observations will justify.

First. In the year 1773, I sailed North 81°, when I was much incommoded with large fields of ice, but the air was not sensibly different there from what I found it a few more degrees Southerly.

Second. I have for many years used the Greenland Fishery; and have, by experience, found those seas the least incumbered with ice betwixt the forepart of May till July.

Third. The same year I sailed to the latitude above mentioned, I found in May, to the West of Spitzbergen, a fine open sea, the wind then blowing South West, and the sea (as far as I could observe from the mast-head) was little incumbered with ice, which fully convinced me that there was a probability of proceeding to a very high latitude.

Fourth. I have observed, that let the wind blow from what quarter it will, it is at times impregnated with frost, snow, &c.; but when most so I am not able to determine. As for rain, I do not recollect ever seeing any there. The weather I have generally found mildest when the wind blows Southerly. As for periodical winds, I do not suppose there are any in Greenland.

IV.

FROM CAPTAIN JOHN GREENSHAW.

In regard to the Queries sent to me, all I have to say is, that if a passage to the North Pole is ever to be accomplished, my opinion is, it must be obtained by going betwixt Greenland and Nova Zembla, as I myself have been to the Westward of Greenland, and reached so far to the Northward as 82° of North Latitude, and to the North and North West of that found nothing but a solid body of ice : my opinion, therefore, is, that it is impossible ever to obtain a passage that way. Captain John Cracroft, in the South Sea Company's time*, was once so far as 83° North Latitude, and to the Northward of Greenland, and met with nothing but a solid field of ice. And in regard to the winds and weather, it freezes continually ; but the

* The South Sea Company sent a small number of ships, for about nine years, on the Greenland Fishery,

wind from the Southward doth commonly bring rain and thick foggy weather, which is chiefly in the latter end of June and July. If you are to the Northward and Westward of Greenland the wind from the North West and North North West doth always open the ice; but at the same time, if it come to blow any time from that quarter, packs it close in with the land; and the winds from the Southward have the contrary effect.

——◆——

V.

THE QUERIES ANSWERED

BY

ANDREW FISHER,

MASTER OF A GREENLAND SHIP AT HULL,

Who has been Twenty-four Voyages from England to the Greenland Seas.

First. Said Andrew Fisher says, that in the year 1746, being on board the ship Ann and Elizabeth from London, on a voyage to the

Greenland Seas, he steered from Hakluyt's
Headland in Spitzbergen North and North
West in clear water till they were in latitude
82° 34′, where they met with a loose pack of
ice, and made their fishery, or otherwise they
might have got through that loose ice, and
doubt not, but thàt they might have gone considerably farther North ; they returned, however,
in clear water to Spitzbergen.

Second. Best seasons of the year are, to be
at or near Spitzbergen from the 15th of May to
the 1st of June, though the years differ, and
the laying of the ice exceedingly : some years it
is not possible to get North of 80° ; at other
times you may meet with very little ice, which
is chiefly owing to the weather in winter, and
the winds in April and May.

Third. There is not any reason to suppose,
that there is any permanent ice, either North or
West of Spitzbergen, so far as 90° ; and it hath
been always found, by able and experienced na-

vigators, that there is not near the quantity of ice, nor so liable to set fast to the North of Spitzbergen, as there is to the South of 80° as far as 74°, owing to the continent of America (called Gallampus Land by the sailors) and Spitzbergen, which makes a narrow passage in proportion to what it is to the North of Spitzbergen. The land of America is sometimes seen by our Greenland Traders from latitude 74° to 76°; and, as it is not seen any farther North, is supposed to round away to the North West, which makes it imagined by many, that there is not any land near the Pole.

Fourth. South winds bring most snow; North winds bring frost; but that is in the month of April and two-thirds of May; after that time, to the 1st or 10th of July, it is in general mild, fine, clear, sunshine weather, and winds variable; after that again, often thick fogs and high winds.

Fifth. It is very possible, by steering North

or North North East by the ship's compass (if
it can be so contrived as to have the card on
the needle steady, and the winds prove favourable), with a little perseverance, a ship may get
near the Pole, if they do not meet with rocks.

———◆———

VI.

SIR,

IN the year 1766, trade being dull, I
fitted a ship at my sole expense to the Greenland Seas; and the said ship returned with one
fish, eleven feet bone. Finding the trade could
be conducted better in private hands than a
company's, I was induced to send a second ship
in 1767, and as I had other concerns in ship-
ping, thought it most prudent (being brought
up to the sea, and having made an easy fortune
from it) to go a voyage to the Greenland Seas,
to see with my own eyes what chance there
might be of making or losing a fortune. So
sailed from Hull the 14th day of April, in my

ship the British Queen, with an old experienced
Master, and on the 24th and 25th of April was
in the latitude of 72°, catching seals amongst
great quantities of loose ice. As we did not
choose to stay in that latitude, we made the best
of our way North; and after sailing through
loose ice, which is commonly the case, about the
6th of May we were as far North as latitude 80°
(which is near what the Masters call *a fishing
latitude*) and about fifteen leagues West of
Hakluyt's Headland. I found the farther North
the less quantity of ice; and from the inquiry I
made, both from the English and Dutch, which
was very considerable, there is a great probability of ships going to the Pole, if not stopped
by meeting land or rocks. It appeared to me,
that the narrowest place in those seas was betwixt
Spitzbergen and the American shore, where the
current is observed to come always from the
North, which fills this narrow place with ice,
but in general loose and floating in the summer,
though I believe congealed and permanent in
winter. Those from whom I inquired informed

me, that the sea was abundantly clearer to the
North of Spitzbergen, and the farther North the
clearer. This seems to prove a wide ocean and
a great opening to the North, as the current comes
from thence, that fills this passage as aforesaid.
The best method of reaching the highest latitude
in my opinion is, to hire two vessels of about
two hundred and fifty tons burthen each, and if
done on a frugal scheme, the same ships might
be fitted for the whale fishery, and premiums
given both for the use of the ship and crew, in
proportion to their approach to the Pole, which,
from many circumstances that may intervene,
might be two or three years before they could
complete their wishes. And it is more likely
they might make their fishery sooner than to the
Southward ; as, if they met with ice, the fish
would be undisturbed ; if clear water and a good
wind, they very soon might reach the Pole.
What I mean by two vessels is, one to foresail
the other at the distance of three or four leagues,
as the latter may avoid the dangers the first
might run into ; and to be always ready, on

seeing and hearing proper signals, to aid and assist, and by that means secure a retreat. I am also of opinion, that such ships being sent on discoveries are much more likely to succeed than his majesty's ships and officers. The above hints I have pointed out for your consideration; and, if I can be of any farther service, may command,

Sir,

Your most humble Servant,

SAM. STANDIDGE.

Hull,
March 4, 1774.

I take this opportunity of laying before the Public the following letter from Captain Marshall, Master of a Greenland Ship, to Captain Heath of the 41st Regiment, who formerly made two voyages to Spitzbergen.

Sir,

In compliance with your request of Wednesday last, I acquaint you, that six years ago I was as high as 82° 30′ North Latitude,

by observation, which is the highest I have ever
been in ; at that time I was Mate of the Royal
Exchange Greenlandman, of Newcastle. I do
not know of any one who has been in a higher
degree; but it has been reported at Newcastle
(with what truth I cannot say), that Captain
Greenshaw, of London, had told his friends,
that he had been as high North as 84°.

The Dutch, I have been informed, have
proceeded to 83° 30′; but I have it only by
hearsay.

In respect to your second Query, I remember, that about five years since, when I was
master of the above-mentioned ship, I was
in 81° North Latitude, by observation,
when there was a clear sea to the Northward, as far as the eye could reach from the
mast head ; and I could not help observing to
my people, that if it had happened that we
were then upon discovery, we might have had
a fine run to the North, as the wind blew fresh
at South. The like clear sea I have observed
several times during the time I have been in

the Greenland Service, which is now about
twenty-one years. I have no doubt but that
a navigator might reach a higher latitude than
I have been in, provided he was well acquainted
with the currents and the ice, for much depends
thereon, and took the advantage of a favourable season. I have remarked, that when the
frost has been severe in England, and to the
Southward *, there has been a great deal less
ice to the Northward the ensuing summer than
usual; and the weather has been remarkably
fine in Greenland. I have, for this reason,
great expectations that the approaching season
will produce a successful fishery, and that it
will also afford an opportunity for a trial to
reach the Pole †.

But the greatest difficulty attending a navi-

* I conceive that this arises from the ice becoming of a
greater thickness during such severe winters, and consequently cannot be so soon broken up, or observed by the
Greenland Ships, which return to the Southward, before
the ice can have floated to them in the Spitzbergen Seas.

† I am sorry to have been informed, since the Bill for
promoting Discoveries passed, that the attempts to penetrate

gator in very high latitudes is how to get back again, for, should he be beset there in the ice, his situation would be very dangerous; for he might be detained a long time, if not for the whole winter. I speak this from experience, for I was once beset for three months, and was given up for lost, and with difficulty got out.

Any farther information in respect to the land, the currents, ice, or other particulars, you may wish to have, I shall very readily communicate it, and am,

Sir,

Your very humble Servant,

JAMES MARSHALL.

No. 5, Spring Street, Shadwell,
February 25, 1776.

Captain Heath, to whom I am indebted for

to the Northward will not be so frequent as I had flattered myself; because, most of the Greenland vessels being insured, if any accident should happen to a ship which is not prosecuting the Whale Fishery, the owners will not be entitled to recover.

this communication, also informs me, that on
the 15th of December, 1777, he minuted the
following particulars from a person employed in
the Whale Fishery.

"That being on board the Prince Frederick
of Liverpool in 1765, commanded by James
Bisbrown, he reached the latitude of 83° 40′,
where he was beset in ice for three weeks to
the Southward, but that he saw, during this
time, an open sea to the North."

The Astronomer Royal having been so good
as to furnish me with the following memorandum, which he made at the time it bears
date, I here subjoin it, as a well authenticated
instance of a navigator's having reached $84\frac{1}{2}°$
of Northern Latitude.

"Mr. Stephens, who went many voyages
to the East Indies, and made much use of the
lunar method of finding the longitude, in
which he is very expert, tells me, this 16th of
March, 1773, that he was formerly two voyages

on the Greenland Fishery ; that, in the second, in the year 1754, he was driven off Spitzbergen, together with a Dutch Ship, by a South South East Wind, North North Westerly by compass into latitude $84\frac{1}{2}°$, or within $5\frac{1}{2}°$ of the Pole, in which latitude he was near the end of the month of May. They saw no land after leaving Hakluyt's Headland (or the Northernmost part of Spitzbergen), and were back in the month of June. Did not find the cold excessive, and used little more than common clothing; met with but little ice, and the less the farther they went to the Northward : met with no drift-wood. It is always clear weather with a North Wind, and thick weather with a Southerly Wind ; nevertheless they could take the sun's altitude for the latitude most days. The sea is quite smooth among the ice, as in the river Thames, and so they also found it to the North of Spitzbergen. Met with no ice higher than the ship's gunnel. Imagines it would hardly have been colder under the Pole, than they experienced it; although he thinks the cold rather increased on going Northward. Thinks the currents are very variable, and have no certain or constant direction. Says he has often tasted the ice, when the sea water has been let to run or dry off it, and always found it fresh. That the sea water will freeze against the ship's bows and rigging, but he never saw it freeze in the ship. That it never freezes in the pumps. A little piece of ice detained under a large piece of ice, when it gets loose from it and comes up to the surface of the water, is very dangerous, it emerging with a force which will sometimes knock a hole in the bottom of the ship. The Dutch Ship which was driven with theirs from Spitzbergen ran against a large piece of ice, and was lost, the ships being then separated to a considerable distance. The winds in these seas are generally Northerly; the Southerly Winds are commonly damp and cold."

Having thus stated the memorandum as I received it from Dr. Maskelyne, I shall now make some observations on the contents.

It appears, by the preceding pages, that, in
this same year, viz. 1754, both Mr. Ware and
Mr. Adams* sailed to $82\frac{1}{2}°$ and 83° during
the month of June, and both of them conceived that they might have reached the North
Pole.

Mr. Maister, by letter from Hull, dated
February 24, 1777, hath procured me the
following information from a friend of his, who,
at my desire, inquired at Whitby with regard
to any ships having reached high Northern
Latitudes.

" Captain Brown of the Freelove says, that,
in the year 1770, he was certainly in 82° North
Latitude, when the water was clear. Captain
Cole also of the Henrietta says, that in 1776
he was near the latitude of 81° North, and after
he was certain of being in that latitude, he was
with strong South East Gales, drove for three
days to the Northward, but as he had thick
weather, the distance was uncertain. In the

* See the Probability of reaching the North Pole,
p. 42, &c.

course of this drift he met with nothing but loose ice."

It appears also by the above account, that Mr. Stephens had proceeded as far as $84\frac{1}{2}°$, the sea being open to the Northward a month earlier in this same year. From this, and other facts of the same kind, I cannot but infer, that the attempt should be made early in the season; if I am right also in what I have before supposed, that the ice, which often packs near the coasts of Spitzbergen, comes chiefly from the rivers, which empty themselves into the Tartarian Sea, it seems highly probable, that this is the proper time of pushing to the Northward, as the ice in such rivers cannot be then completely broken up. What other ice therefore may be seen at this time is probably the remains of what was disembogued during the preceding summer.

Another proof of this arises from what happened in 1778, for the Carcase and Race Horse were obstructed, at $80\frac{1}{2}°$, by an immense bank

of ice, during part of the months of July and
August; but four Greenland Masters were a
degree farther to the Northward, during the
months of May and June, in the same year *.

No one winters in Spitzbergen, but some few
Russians, from whom however we have not
been informed what happens during that season,
though it should seem, from the observations of
Barentz, those of the Russians in Maloy Brun,
and a ship having pushed into the Atlantic, from
Hudson's Bay, during the midst of December †,
that the Northern Seas are then navigable.

For the same reason, probably, Clipperton‡,
who passed the Straits of Magellan in the
midst of winter, saw no ice, which is so frequently met with at Midsummer by those who
sail to the Southward of Cape Horn.

* See the Probability of reaching the North Pole, p. 4,
45, 46, and 57.

† See the Probability of reaching the North Pole, p 83.

‡ Frezier was as far South as 58° in the middle of May,
and saw no ice, though he speaks of a South East Wind as
cold.—See Callander's Collection of Voyages, vol. iii,
p. 461.

I take this opportunity of recapitulating the years since 1746*, during which it appears, from the instances I have stated, that the sea to the North of Spitzbergen hath been open, so as to permit attempts of approaching the Pole, which will show that such opportunities are not uncommon, and it is hoped that they will be more frequently embraced, from a parliamentary reward of five thousand pounds being given to such of his majesty's subjects as shall first penetrate beyond the 89th degree of Northern Latitude; the Bill for which purpose hath already passed both Houses of Parliament†.

* Viz. 1746, 1751, 1752, 1754, 1756, 1759, 1763, 1765, 1766, 1769, 1771, and 1773.

† By the same Bill, a reward of twenty thousand pounds is given to such of his majesty's subjects as shall first discover a communication between the Atlantic and Pacific Oceans, in any direction whatsoever of the Northern Hemisphere.

AS it appears, by the two first collections of instances, that I have had much conversation
with the officers of the Royal Navy, as well as
masters of Greenland Ships, about a Polar
Voyage, I shall now state several hints which
have occasionally dropped from them, with regard to prosecuting discoveries to the Northward.

The ship should be such as is commonly
used in the Greenland Fishery, or rather of a
smaller size, as it works the more readily when
the ice begins to pack around it.

There should, on no account, be a larger
complement of men than can be conveniently
stowed in the boats, as it sometimes happens,
that the Greenland Vessels are lost in the ice ;
but the crews generally escape by means of their
boats. The crew also should consist of a larger
proportion of smiths and carpenters than are
usually put on board common ships,

As it may happen, that the crews in boats may be kept a considerable time before they can reach either ship or shore, there should be a sort of awning to be used occasionally, if the weather should prove very inclement.

As it is not wanted that the boats should last many years, it is advised, that they should be built of the lightest materials, because, on this account, they are more easily dragged over the packed ice *.

As it is possible, also, that the crew may be obliged to winter within the Arctic Circle, it is recommended that the ship should be ballasted with coals.

That there should be a framed house of

* General Oglethorpe informs me, that the Dutch Vessels on the Greenland Fishery have three boats fastened on each side of the ship, which may be sufficient to contain the whole crew in case of accidents; and that the early discoverers had always what was called *a ship in quarters* on board, which might be put together when a creek, &c. was to be explored. He also advises, that the sailing of the two ships, to be sent in concert on discoveries, should be previously tried, as there should not be too great a disparity in that circumstance.

wood on board, to be made as long as possible, for the opportunity of exercise within doors *.

That there should be also a Russian Stove, as a fire in a common chimney does not warm the room equably.

It appears, by the accounts of the Dutch, who wintered in Nova Zembla †, as well as the Russians, who continued six years in Maloy Brun, that during this season there are sometimes days of a tolerable temperature ; snow shoes, therefore, should be provided, as also snow eyes, not to lose the benefit of air and exercise during such an interval ‡. The beard,

* On the Labrador Coast, the furriers raise a wall of earth all round their huts, as high as the roof, which is found to contribute much to warmth within doors, so as to want little more heat than arises from the steam of lamps. Such wall is commonly three feet thick.

† The Russian Hereticks, *of the old faith,* as they are stiled, sometimes winter in Nova Zembla. — Account of Maloy Brun.

‡ A barrelled organ, which plays a few country dances, might amuse during the dark months, as also be of use in the first intercourse with the savages, musick being a sort of universal language ; and Sir Francis Drake, for that reason, carried out musicians with him.

likewise, should be suffered to grow on the approach of winter, from which the Russian Couriers are enabled to support the severity of the open air.

Russian boots, and the winter cap of the furriers of North America, are also recommended; but recourse should not be had to this warmest clothing upon the first approach of winter, for by these means the Russians do not commonly endure cold so well as the English; because when the weather becomes excessively severe, they cannot well add to their warmth.

When the weather is very inclement, leads for the hands, dumb bells, and other such exercises, should be contrived for within-doors.

In order to prevent the scurvy, likewise, frequent use of the flesh-brush is recommended, as also occasionally a warm bath, from which James's crew received great benefit, when they wintered on Charlton Island.

With regard to the provisions, I shall here insert a method of curing meat, communicated to me by Admiral Sir Charles Knowles, the good effects of which both himself and others have frequently experienced *.

* So soon as the ox is killed, let it be skinned and cut up into pieces, fit for use, as quick as possible, and salted whilst the meat is hot; for which purpose, have a sufficient quantity of saltpetre and bay salt pounded together, and made hot in an oven, of each equal parts; with this sprinkle the meat, at the rate of about two ounces to the pound. Then lay the pieces on shelving boards to drain for twenty-four hours; which done, turn them and repeat the same operation, and let them lay for twenty-four hours longer, by which time the salt will be all melted, and have penetrated the meat, and the juices be drained off. Each piece must then be wiped dry with clean coarse cloths, and a sufficient quantity of common salt, made hot likewise in an oven, and mixed (when taken out) with about one-third brown sugar. The casks being ready, rub each piece well with this mixture, and pack them well down, allowing half a pound of the salt and sugar to each pound of meat, and it will keep good several years.

N. B. It is best to proportion the casks or barrels to the quantity consumed at a time, as the seldomer the meat is exposed to the air the better. The same process does for pork, only a larger quantity of salt, and less sugar; but the preservation of both equally depends on the meat's being hot when first salted. Sir John Narborough salted young seals, and Sir Richard Hawkins many barrels of penguins, both of which are said to have been wholesome and palatable: fish likewise caught at the approach of winter might

The flour should be kiln-dried, and put into tight barrels which are capable of holding liquids *. Flour thus preserved and packed hath been perfectly good for more than three years, without the least appearance of the weevils.

To make the best use of flour thus preserved, there should be both a biscuit maker and an oven on board.

With regard to liquors, a large quantity of shrub from the best spirits and fruits is recommended, which should also be made just before the voyage takes place; the stronger the spirit, the less stowage. Dampier preferred Vidonia to other wines, on account of its acidity; and perhaps old hock might still answer better.

I should stand in need of many apologies,

be so cured, or indeed preserved by the frost without any salt. Captain Cook's precautions need not be here alluded to.

* Woodes Rogers observes in his voyage, that the water, which he had brought with him from England, on his arrival at Juan Fernandez, was all spoiled by the casks being bad. —Callander, iii, p. 259.

for having suggested these hints to Northern Discoverers, had I not received them from officers of the Royal Navy, as well as Greenland Masters, and eminent physicians; if any of these particulars, however, would not have been otherwise thought of upon fitting out the ship for such a voyage, and should be attended with any good effects, it will become my best excuse.

In order also to promote such a voyage of discovery, I should conceive that extending the parliamentary reward of twenty thousand pounds by 18 Geo. II, cap. 17, for the passage to the Pacific Ocean through Hudson's Bay, to a Northern communication between the Atlantic and Pacific Oceans in any direction whatsoever, might greatly contribute to the attempting such an enterprize.

To this, another incitement might be perhaps added, by given one thousand pounds for every degree of Northern latitude, which might be reached by the adventurer from 85° to the Pole, as some so very peremptorily deny all former instances of having penetrated to such high latitudes. An act hath accordingly passed for the first of these purposes ; and, for the second, with this variation, that a reward of five thousand pounds is given only for approaching within a degree of the Pole.

I shall conclude, however, in answer to their incredulity by the following citation from Hakluyt : —

" Now, lest you should make small account of ancient writers, or of their experience, which travelled before our times, reckoning their authority amongst fables of no importance, I have, for the better assurance of those proofs, set down part of a discourse written in the Saxon tongue, and translated into English by Mr. Nowel, servant to master secretary Cecil, wherein is described a navigation, which one Ochter made in the time of King Alfred, king of West Saxe, anno 871 ; the words of which discourse are these : ' He sailed right North, having always the desert land on the starboard, and on the larboard the main sea, continuing his course till he perceived the coast bowed directly towards

the East, &c.' Whereby it appeareth, that he
went the same way that we do now yearly trade
by St. Nicholas into Muscovia, which no man
in our age knew for certainty to be sea, till it
was again discovered by the English in the
time of Edward VI.

" Nevertheless, if any man should have taken
this voyage in hand, by the encouragement of
this only author *, he should have been thought

---

* Perhaps the same sea is alluded to in the following
line of Dionysius :—

Ποντον μεν καλευσι, πεπηγοία, κρονιον, τε.

as the name of *Frozen* can scarcely be applied to that of the
Baltic.

As for the Thule of the ancients, about which so many
conjectures have been made, it seems to have most clearly
been Ireland, from the manner in which Statius addresses a
Poem to Crispinus, whose father had carried the Emperor's
commands to Thule :—

—— tu disce patrem, quantusque nigrantem
Fluctibus *occiduis, fessoq. Hyperione* Thulen
Intrâvit *mandata* gerens.

It should also seem, from other parts of the same Poem,
that this General had crossed from Scotland to the North of
Ireland, or Thule :—

Quod si te magno tellus *frænata* parenti
Accipiat, quantum ferus exultabit Araxes?

but simple, considering that this navigation was written so many years past, in so barbarous a tongue, by one only obscure author; and yet in these our days, we find by our own experience his reports to be true."

Quanta Caledonios attollet gloria campos?
Cum tibi longævus referet trucis incola terræ,
Hic suetus dare jura parens, hoc cespite turmas
Affari; nitidas speculas, castellaque longé.
Aspicis? ille dedit cinxitque hæc moenia fossâ.

STATIUS, v. 14.

Crispinus's father, therefore, must have resided some time in Scotland, from whence he went to Thule or Ireland, for the Hebrides (the only land to the West except Ireland) could not have been of sufficient consequence for the Emperor's commision, or the fortifications alluded to ; besides that the expression of *fessoque Hyperione* implies, that the land lay considerably to the Westward.

I

THOUGHTS

ON THE

PROBABILITY, EXPEDIENCY, AND UTILITY,

OF

DISCOVERING A PASSAGE

BY

THE NORTH POLE*.

THE possibility of making discoveries in this way (that is, by steering directly North), though now treated as paradoxical by many, was not, as will hereafter appear, formerly looked upon in that light, even by such as ought to be reputed the properest judges. There have been a

---

* I have lately received these reflections from a learned friend, who is now deceased, and who permitted me to print them, though not to inform the public to whom they are indebted for this very valuable communication.

D. B———.

variety of causes, that, at different times, have
retarded undertakings of the utmost importance
to the human species. Among these we may
justly consider the conduct of some great philosophers, who, as our judicious Verulam wisely
observes, quitting the luminous path of experience to investigate the operations of nature by
their own speculations, imposed upon the bulk
of mankind specious opinions for incontestable
truths; which, being propagated by their disci-
ples through a long series of years, captivated
the minds of men, and thereby deprived them
of that great instrument of science, the spirit of
inquiry*. In succeeding ages a new impediment arose, from the setting up profit as the
ultimate object of discovery; and then, as
might well be expected, the preferring the
private and particular gain of certain individuals to the general interests of the community,
as well as to the interest of the whole world, in

---

* Baconi Opera, tom. iv, p. 100; *et alibi passim.* But
these passages may be found collected in Shaw's Abridg-
ment of Bacon's Works, vol. ii, p. 52.

the extension of science. This it was that induced the States General, at the instance of
their East India Company, to discourage all
attempts for finding a North East Passage, and
to stifle such accounts as tended to show that
it was practicable. We may add to these, the
sourness of disappointed navigators, who endeavoured to render their own miscarriages
proofs of the impracticability of any like attempts.
This was the case of Captain Wood, who was
shipwrecked upon Nova Zembla, and who declared that all endeavours on that side were,
and would be found vain ; though Barentz,
who died there in a like expedition, affirmed,
with his last breath, that, in his own opinion,
such a passage might be found.

That the Earth was spherical in its form was
an opinion very early entertained, and amongst
the learned generally admitted. It seemed to
be a plain deduction from thence, that a right
line, passing through the globe, would terminate
in two points diametrically opposite. Plato is
thought to be the first who spoke of the inhabitants (if such there were) dwelling at or near

those points by the name of Antipodes. This doctrine occasioned disputes among philosophers for many ages ; some maintained, some denied, and some treated it as absurd, ridiculous, and impossible *. Whoever will examine impartially the sentiments of these great men, weigh the contrariety of their opinions, and consider the singularity of their reasonings, will see and be convinced how unsatisfactory their notions were, and discover from thence, how insufficient the subtle speculations of the human understanding are towards settling points like these, when totally unassisted by the lights of observation and actual experience.

The division of the globe by zones being agreeable to nature, the ancients distinguished them very properly and accurately into two frigid, the Arctic and Antarctic Circles ; two temperate, lying between those circles and the tropics ; and the torrid zone within the tropics, equally divided by the equinoctial. But judging

* Lucr. de Natura Rerum, lib i, ver. 1063 ; Cicer. Acad. Quæst. lib. iv ; Plin. Hist. Nat. lib. ii, cap. 65 ; Plut. de Facie in Orbe Lunæ ; Macrob. de Somn. Scip. lib. ii.

from their experience of the nature of the climates at the extremities of the zone which they
inhabited, they concluded, that the frigid zones
were utterly uninhabitable from cold, and the
torrid from intolerable heat of the sun. Pliny
laments very pathetically upon this supposition,
that the race of mankind were pent up in so
small a part of the Earth. The poets, who were
also no despicable philosophers, heightened the
horrors of these inhospitable regions by all the
colouring of a warm and heated imagination * ;
but we now know, with the utmost certainty,
that they were entirely mistaken as to both.
For within the Arctic Circle there are countries
inhabited as high nearly as we have discovered;
and, if we may confide in the relations of those
who have been nearest the Pole✝, the heat
there is very considerable, in respect to which

* Cicero in Somnium Scipionis; Virg. Georg. lib. i;
Ovidii Met. lib. i; Tibullus Panegyr. ad Messalam, lib. iv;
Plin. Hist. Nat. lib. ii, cap. 68; Pomp. Mela de Situ
Orbis, lib. i, cap. 1; Claud. de Raptu Proserpinæ,
lib. i.

✝ That the Earth had inhabitants, even under the
Poles, seems to have been believed by many at the

our own navigators and the Dutch perfectly
agree.   In regard to the torrid zone, we have
now not the least doubt of its being thoroughly
inhabited ; and, which is more wonderful, that
the climates are very different there, according
to the circumstances of their situation.   In
Ethiopia, Arabia, and the Moluccas, exceedingly hot; but in the plains of Peru (and particular at Quito) perfectly temperate, so that
the inhabitants never-change their clothes in
any season of the year.   The sentiments of the
ancients therefore-in this respect are a proof
how inadequate the faculties of the human mind
are to discussions of this nature, when unassisted
by facts.

The Pythagorean system of the universe, re-

latter end of the sixteenth century, from the following
lines : —

"Fond men! if we believe that men do live
    Under the zenith of both frozen poles,
Though none come thence advertisements to give,
    Why bear we not the like faith of our souls?"

                          Sir John Davis's *Nosce te ipsum*,
probably written in 1596, from a compliment to Lord
Keeper Egerton on his first receiving the Great Seal.

                                        D. B———.

vised and restored near two hundred and fifty years ago by the celebrated Copernicus, met with a very difficult and slow reception, not only from the bulk of mankind, for that might have been well expected, but even from the learned; and some very able astronomers attempted to overturn and refute it *. Galileo Galilei wrote an admirable treatise in its support, in which he very fully removed most of the popular objections †. This, however, exposed him to the rigour of the inquisition, and he was obliged to abjure the doctrine of the Earth's motion. Our noble phi-

---

* Amongst the most considerable of these was John Baptist Riccioli, who published his *Almagestum Novum* with this view. Yet afterwards, in his *Astronomia Reformata*, he found himself obliged to have recourse to the doctrine of the Earth's motion, that he might be able to give his calculations with a proper degree of exactness.

† This celebrated work of his was entitled, *Dialoghi de Sistemi di Tolomeo, e di Copernico.* This is much better known to the learned world by a Latin translation, which so clearly proved the superiority of the Copernican System, that the only means of refuting it was by the censures of the church.

losopher, the deep and acute Lord Verulam, could not absolutely confide in the truth and certainty of the Copernican System; but seems to think, that its facilitating astronomical calculations was its principal recommendation, as if this had not been also a very strong presumption at least, if not a proof, of its veracity *. It was from this consideration that the church of Rome at length thought fit so far to relax in her decisions, as to permit the maintaining the Earth's motion in physical and philosophical disquisitions. But Sir Isaac Newton, who built upon this basis his experimental philosophy, hath dispersed all doubts on this subject, and shown how the most sublime discoveries may be made by the reciprocal aids of sagacity and observation. On these grounds, therefore, all inquiries of this nature ought to proceed, without paying an implicit submission to the mere speculative notions even of the greatest men; but pursuing steadily the path of truth,

* Shaw's Abridgement of Bacon's Works, vol ii, p. 21, where the Doctor endeavours to defend this opinion. 1

under the direction of the light of experience.

It may be urged, in excuse of the ancients, and even of our ancestors in former times, that, as they were unassisted by facts, they could only employ guess and conjecture, and that consequently their conclusions were from thence erroneous. But to wave the visible impropriety of deciding in points, where observation was so obviously necessary, without its direction, let us see whether this plea of alleviation may not be controverted in both cases. Cornelius Nepos reports, that some Indians being cast on shore in Germany were sent by a prince of the Suevi to Quintus Metellus Celer, then the Roman proconsul in Gaul*. A very learned writer, in discussing this point, hath shown, that it was possible for these Indians to have come by two different routes into the Baltic. He thinks, however, that it is very improbable they came by either, and supposes, that they were either Nor-

---

* Plin. Hist. Nat. lib. ii, cap. 67.

wegians, or some other wild people, to whom, from their savage appearance, they gave the name of Indians *. But though this observation may well enough apply to the Romans, who at that time had no knowledge of these Northern People, yet it is not easy to conceive, that the Suevi could fall into this mistake; or, if they did not, that they should attempt to impose upon the Romans. It appears incontestably, that, in the time of King Alfred, the Northern Seas were constantly navigated upon the same motives they are now; that is, for the sake of catching whales and sea-horses. Nicholas of Lynn, a Carmelite Friar, sailed to the most distant islands in the North, and even as high as the Pole. He dedicated an account of his discoveries to King Edward the Third, and was certainly a person of great learning, and an able

* Huet Histoire de Commerce, et de la Navigation des Anciens, p. 531.

† See Barrington's Translation of Orosius from the Anglo-Saxon of King Alfred, part ii, p. 9.

astronomer *, if we may believe the celebrated Chaucer, who, in his Treatise on the Astrolabe, mentions him with great respect.

After Columbus discovered America, under the auspices of Ferdinand and Isabella, the Sovereigns of Europe, and especially Henry the Seventh, turned their thoughts towards and gave great encouragement to discoveries. Mr. Robert Thorne, who resided many years as a merchant in Spain, and who was afterwards mayor of Bristol, wrote a letter to Henry the Eighth, in which he strongly recommended a voyage to the North Pole. He gave his reasons more at large in a long Memorial to our ambassador in Spain, which show him to have been a very judicious man, and for those times

---

* Leland. Comment. de Script. Britan. cap. 370; Bale, vi, 25; Pits, p. 505. His description was intituled, *Inventio Fortunata;* besides which, he wrote, amongst other things, a book, *De Mundi Revolutione,* which possibly may still remain in the Bodleian Library. This Friar, as Dr. Dee asserts, made five voyages into these Northern Parts, and left an account of his discoveries from the latitude of 54° to the Pole.

a very able cosmographer; and accompanied
this Memorial with a Map of the World, to
prove the practicability of his proposal *.
Though this project of his was not attended to,
yet a variety of expeditions were made for discovering a passage by the North West, and
others by the North East, into the South Seas
on the one side, and into the Tartarian Ocean on
the other, until at length both were declared impracticable by Captain James and Captain Wood;
soured by their own miscarriages, and being
strongly persuaded, that, as they did not succeed,
none else could. But even these unsuccessful
voyages were not unprofitable to the nation upon
the whole, as they opened a passage to many lu-
crative fisheries, such as those in Davis's Straits,
Baffin's Bay, and on the coast of Spitzbergen.
Besides this, they laid open Hudson's Straits
and Bay with the coast on both sides, which

* Hakluyt's Voyages, vol. i, p. 212—220. The Letter
to Dr. Ley, who was the King's Ambassador in Spain, is
dated A. D. 1527. This Mr. Thorne's father was engaged,
with others, in the discovery of Newfoundland.

have been already productive of many advantages, and which, in process of time, cannot fail of producing more, in consequence of our being in possession of Canada, and being thereby sole master of those seas and coasts.

It is, however, very remarkable, that notwithstanding the views, both of our traders and of such great men as were distinguished encouragers of discoveries, the ablest seamen (who without doubt are the best judges) were still inclined to this passage by the North, such as Captain Poole, Sir William Monson *, and others; and this was still the more remarkable, as they were entirely guided therein by the lights of their own experience, having no knowledge of Mr. Thorne's proposal, or of the sentiments of each other. From the reason of the thing, however, they uniformly concurred in the motives they suggested for such an undertaking. They asserted, that this passage would be much shorter and easier than any of those

* Naval Tracts, p. 435.

by the North West or North East; that it
would be more healthy for the seamen, and
attended with fewer inconveniences; that it
would probably open a passage to new countries; and, finally, that the experiment might
be made with very little hazard, at a small
expense, and would redound highly to our
national honour, if attended with success. It
may be then demanded, why it has not hitherto
been attempted, and what objections have retarded a scheme so visibly advantageous?
The objections, as far as they can be collected,
are the fear of perishing by excessive cold, the
danger of being blocked up in ice, and the
apprehension that there could be no certainty of
preserving the use of the compass under or near
the Pole.

In respect to the first, we have already mentioned, that the ancients had taken up an opinion, that the seas in the frigid zone were im-
passable, and the lands, if there were any, uninhabitable. The philosophers of later ages fell
into the same opinion, and maintained, that the

Poles were the sources and principles of cold, which of course increased and grew excessive in approaching them *. But when the lights of experience were admitted to guide in such researches, the truth of this notion came to be questioned, because from facts it became probable, that there might be a diversity of climates in the frigid as well as in the torrid zone. Charlton Island, in which Captain James wintered, lies in the bottom, that is, in the most Southern part of Hudson's Bay, and in the same latitude with Cambridge, and the cold there was intolerable. The servants of the Hudson's Bay Company trade annually in places ten degrees nearer the Pole, without feeling any such inconvenience. The city of Moscow is in the same latitude with that of Edinburgh, and yet in winter the weather is almost as severe there as in Charlton Island.

* In the language of those times, the Pole was stiled *Primum Frigidum;* and it was by such groundless phrases that men pretended to account for the operations of nature, without giving themselves the trouble of experimental inquiries.

K

Nova Zembla hath no soil, herbage, or animals; and yet in Spitzbergen, in six degrees higher latitude, there are all three ; and, on the top of the mountains in the most Northern part, men strip themselves of their shirts that they may cool their bodies *. The celebrated Mr. Boyle, from these and many other instances, rejected the long received notion, that the Pole was the principle of cold. Captain Jonas Poole, who in 1610 sailed in a vessel of seventy tons to make discoveries towards the North, found the weather warm in near 79° of latitude, whilst the ponds and lakes were unfrozen, which put him in hopes of finding a mild summer, and led him to believe, that a passage might be as soon found by the Pole as any other way whatever ; and for this reason, that the sun gave a great heat there, and that the ice was not near so thick as what he had met with in the latitude of 73°†. Indeed, the Dutchmen, who pretend to have advanced

---

* See Marden's Account of Spitzbergen, p. 105.

† Purchas's Pilgrims, vol. iii, p. 702.

within a degree of the Pole, said it was as hot there as in the summer at Amsterdam.

In these Northern Voyages we hear very much of ice, and there is no doubt that vessels are very much hindered and incommoded thereby. But after all, it is, in the opinion of able and experienced seamen, more formidable in appearance than fatal in its effects. When our earliest discoveries were made, and they reached farther North than we commonly sail at present, it was performed in barks of seventy tons, with some trouble, no doubt, but with very little hazard. At this day it is known, that in no part of the world there are greater quantities of ice seen than in Hudson's Bay, and yet there is no navigation safer, the company not losing a ship in twenty years, and the seamen, who are used to it, are not troubled with any apprehensions about it. It is no objection to this, that we hear almost every season of ships lost in the ice on the Whale Fishery; for these vessels, instead of avoiding, industriously seek the ice, as amongst it the whales are more commonly

found than in the open sea. Being thus continually amongst the ice, it is no wonder that
they are sometimes surrounded by it; and yet
the men, when the ships are lost, generally
speaking, escape. But in the seas near the
Pole, it is very probable, there is little or no
ice, for that is commonly formed in bays and
rivers during winter, and does not break up and
get into the sea till the latter end of March, or
the beginning of April, when it begins to thaw
upon the shores. It is also, when formed, very
uncertain as to its continuance, being broken
and driven about by the vehemence of the
winds. As a proof of this we have an instance
of a vessel frozen in one of the harbours of
Hudson's Bay, which, by the breaking of the
ice, drove to sea, and, though it was Christmas,
found the Straits quite free from ice *, which
are frequently choked with it in May and
June, and made a safe and speedy passage
home. All our accounts agree, that, in very

* Mr. Dobbs's Account of Hudson's Bay, p. 69, 70.

high latitudes, there is less ice. Barentz, when his ship was frozen in Nova Zembla, heard the ice broken with a most horrible noise by an impetuous sea from the North, a full proof that it was open. It is the invariable tradition of the Samoides and Tartars, who live beyond the Waygat, that the sea is open to the North of Nova Zembla all the year; and the most knowing people in Russia are of the same opinion. These authorities ought certainly to have more weight than simple conjectures.

The notion, that approaching to a passage under the Pole would destroy the use of the compass, is a popular opinion without any just grounds to support it. For it presumes that the needle is directed by the Pole of the World; which it certainly is not, as appears from the needle's variation, and even the variation of that variation, which, if this notion was true, could never happen. In Sir Thomas Smith's Sound in Baffin's Bay the variation was found to be 56° Westward, the greatest yet known. Captain Wood is very clear upon this point, and maintains, that no danger was to be apprehended from this cause *. Those who asserted, that they had advanced within a degree of the Pole, estimated the variation there at five points of the compass. Captain Wood, in stating the account given of the Dutch seamen's voyage by Captain Goulden, omits one very material point, of which we are informed by Mr. Boyle, which is, that one of the Dutch captains coming over to England, Captain Goulden carried him to some of the Northern Company, who were perfectly satisfied as to the truth of his relation†. On the whole, therefore, whether we respect reason or facts, there are no just grounds for apprehensions on this head, more especially as there are other means by which the true situation of a vessel might be determined, and the difficulty, if any arose, would

* Wood's Voyage for the Discovery of a North East Passage, p. 139.

† See the Honourable Mr. Boyle's History of Cold, in respect to this and a multitude of other curious particulars, which show with how much industry and care he struggled to deliver truth from vulgar errors, and fiction.

be but of very short continuance. But as such a voyage could not fail of affording many new lights in respect to astronomy and geography, so in this respect also it must necessarily ascertain fully what is at present only matter of doubt and conjecture.

As notions long received acquire from thence a degree of credit due only to truth; and as new opinions, contrary to these, and in other respects perhaps extraordinary in themselves, meet from these causes with slow and difficult belief, however they may appear to be supported by arguments, authorities, or facts (which it is presumed have been freely and fairly urged in the present case, to a degree that may at least entitle the matter to some attention); let us now proceed one step farther. This shall be to show, that what seems to be so repugnant to the common course of things (*viz.* that near the North Pole the cold should relax, and the ice be less troublesome) is perfectly conformable to the laws of nature, or, which is the same thing, to the will and wisdom of our great Creator. If this can be proved, there can be no farther dispute as to the possibility of this passage; more especially when it shall also appear, that this affords a full solution of all the doubts that have been suggested, and at the same time clearly accounts for, and effectually confirms, the facts and reasonings deduced from them, which have been already advanced upon this subject. To come then at once to the point.

Sir Isaac Newton, who it is universally allowed was equally accurate, cautious, and judicious, in his philosophical decisions, hath demonstrated clearly, that the figure of this our Earth is not spherical, but of an oblate spheroidal form, the diameter at the Equator being the greatest, and at the axis the least of all the lines that can pass through the centre. He also determined, by a most curious calculation, the proportion of these diameters to be as two hundred and thirty to two hundred and twenty-nine. These sentiments of his have been experimentally verified by the means which he also pointed out, viz.

observing the motion of pendulums in very different latitudes, and the actual measurement of a degree at the Equator and under the Arctic Circle. This last evidently proved the depression of the Earth's surface towards the Pole, which no doubt gradually increases. The very learned and sagacious Dr. Hooke asserted, in one of his lectures, and brought very strong reasons to show, that there is nothing but sea at the Poles *. These points then, being maturely considered, will be found to militate in favour of a free passage this way, and at the same time give much light into other things that have been advanced in the course of this inquiry, by showing the true causes of those facts that, at first sight, have appeared to many very strange and unaccountable. For example, if there be no land near the Pole, then there can be no bays in which ice can be formed to interrupt the navigation. Again, the rays of the sun, falling on so flat a surface, and being

* Hooke's Posthumous Works, p. 351.

continually reflected from the water, must afford a great degree of heat to the air. At the same time this will account for the sun's being seen by the Dutch in Nova Zembla a fortnight earlier than he should have appeared, according to astronomical calculations*. Many other circumstances might be mentioned, but these will doubtless occur to the intelligent, and therefore it is unnecessary to dwell longer upon them.

The great injustice of rejecting opinions, on account of their appearing, at first sight, paradoxical, or somewhat inconsistent with notions commonly received, having been clearly shown, and the mischievous consequences flowing from it by various instances pointed out; the foundation of this conjecture, that there may be a passage near the Pole, having been fairly stated, the popular objections to it clearly removed, the general advantage that might be expected from thence placed in a proper

* See Purchas, vol. iii, p. 499, 500.

light, and the consistence of all the circumstances relative thereto, with the established
course of nature, having been also rendered
evident; there can be nothing more looked for
respecting this matter merely in the light of a
philosophical speculation. But if supporting
this had been the only motive, these reflections
had not employed the time of the writer, or
trespassed so long upon the reader's patience.
What then remains? To demonstrate, that, as
the possibility, practicability, and facility, of
such an undertaking have been insisted upon,
its national utility should be shown to deserve
consideration; and that as it is an object of
the greatest importance to the public welfare,
its execution should be no longer delayed.
There is unquestionably no country in Europe
so well situate for such an enterprize as this.
The transit from Shetland to the Northern
parts of Asia would, by this way, be a voyage
only of a few weeks. The inhabitants of these
islands and of the Orkneys are, and have been
for many years, employed in the Greenland

Fisheries, and the natives of these isles are the persons mostly sent to the establishments in Hudson's Bay. By these means they are inured to cold, to ice, and hard living, and are consequently the fittest for being employed in such expeditions. When this shall be once executed with success it will necessarily bring us acquainted with new Northern Countries, where ordinary clothes and other coarse woollen goods will probably be acceptable, new channels of commerce would be thereby opened, our navigation extended, the number of our seamen augmented, without exhausting our strength in settling colonies, exposing the lives of our sailors in tedious and dangerous voyages through unwholesome climates, or having any other trade in prospect than that of exchanging our native commodities and manufactures for those of other countries. This, if it could be brought about, would, in the first instance, convert a number of bleak and barren islands into cultivation, connect them and their inhabitants intimately with Britain, give bread to many thousands, and by providing suitable rewards for many different species of industry, encourage population, and put an easy and effectual period to the mischiefs and scandal of emigrations. The benefits derived from these discoveries, and the commerce arising from them, will necessarily extend to all parts of our dominions. For however fit the poor people of those islands may be for such enterprises, or however commodious the ports in their countries may be found for equipping and receiving vessels employed in these voyages, yet the commodities, manufactures, &c. must be furnished from all parts of the British Empire, and of course be of universal advantage. These, as they are true, will it is hoped appear just and cogent reasons for wishing, that a project, which has dwelt in the mouths and memories of some, and in the judgment and approbation of a few, from the time of Henry the Eighth, should be revived, and, at length, for the benefit of his subjects, carried into effect, under the auspices of George the Third.

I HAVE mentioned in the preceding sheets *, that I expected some additional instances of Dutch Ships, which had been in high Northern Latitudes; but, though I delayed the publication for some weeks, they did not arrive time enough to appear with the others. I have however since received them from Professor Allamand of Leyden, F. R. S. by means of Mr. Valltravers, F. R. S., &c., and take the earliest opportunity to lay them before the public, as a valuable addition to the former papers.

TO THE HONOURABLE DAINES BARRINGTON.

SIR,

HAVING made inquiries (agreeable to your desire) from Professor Allamand of Leyden, F. R. S. with regard to Dutch Navigators, who have reached high Northern Lati-

* In the Additional Papers from Hull, p. 77.

titudes : he has been so kind to send me the following account, drawn up by Captain William May, a very distinguished and experienced Sea Officer, in the Dutch Service, which begins with a letter from Mr. John Walig to his owners, who has been Master of a Greenland Ship ever since the year 1740.

I am, &c.

ROD. VALLTRAVERS.

" TO MESS. NIC. AND JACOB VAN STAPHORST.

Helder, Jan. 3, 1775.

" In answer to your Letter of the 22d of December concerning the question, whether we have been nearer to the Pole than $80\frac{1}{2}^{\circ}$, I must inform you, that we have been often to 81°, near the Seven Islands, to the Northward of the North East Land, and some have been in 82°, but then not clear from ice, in which they drove about. I never heard of any discoveries made there, as they have always been fishers, who, driving with the ice to the Northward, leave that direction upon getting

room ; and when now and then the sea has
been free from ice, that has happened commonly in the months of June and July. In
1763, I spoke with a Scotch Captain in Greenland, who told me he had been to 83°, that the
sea was then free from ice, but that he had
made no discoveries, without mentioning any
more particulars, for we ask after nothing but
whales. When I spoke to him it was in July,
and then we could get no farther North than
79° 30′ for the ice. In short, we can seldom
proceed much higher than $80\frac{1}{2}$°, but almost
always to that latitude, for it seems that the
conjunction of the currents often fastens the ice
there. I fished last year from 80° 25′ to 80° 35′,
according to the land we made afterwards.

" But in the year 1707, Captain Cornelis
Gillis, having gone without any ice far to the
Northward of 81°, sailed to the North of the
Seven Islands, proceeded from thence East, and
afterwards South East, remaining to -the East
of the North East Land, when coming again
to latitude 80° he discovered about twenty-five

miles * East from the country to the North East very High Lands, on which, as far as we know, no body has ever been. As to the season when the Spitzbergen Seas may be expected to be free from ice, I believe, according to my observations, that the most open sea to the Northward generally happens in the month of September, but then the nights begin, and make the navigation dangerous.

" I am, &c.

" JOHN WALIG."

* Fifteen to a degree at the Equator.

A SHORT

ACCOUNT OF NAVIGATORS,

WHO HAVE REACHED

HIGH NORTHERN LATITUDES*.

———◆———

I WENT to Amsterdam the 26th of March, being the most proper time to make the desired inquiries, and to obtain information from all the commanders that were to depart this year to Greenland; for then you meet six, eight, and more together, in houses where they enlist their men. I am, however, sorry to mention, that but few of those commanders keep journals when they are near, or in the ice; but, notwith-standing this, the accounts they give carry with

* This account was drawn up by Captain William May, in the service of the States, at the desire of Professor Allamand of Leyden. — See p. 94.

L 2

them such an air of truth, from being confirmed
by minute circumstances, and corroborated by
so many witnesses, that these relations (I verily
believe) may be depended upon as well as some
journals. I particularly applied myself, however, to those to whom a great number of
voyages had given experience, and (contrary
to my expectations) met with men of candour
and penetration. I thought it proper, likewise, to take the following extract of a Journal,
it showing the common form in which some of
them are kept.

*Translation of part of a Journal, kept on Board
the Vrow Maria, Commander Martin Breet.*

N. B. The sun's altitudes were taken with an
octant, and twelve minutes allowed for the
sun's semi-diameter, refraction, and dip of
the horizon ; the longitude from Teneriffe ;
the miles fifteen to a degree at the equator ;
the bearings with a compass unrectified.

The 22d of April, 1771, sailed from the

Texel for Greenland. 8th of May, latitude, according to the run, 70° 33', longitude 19° 22'; saw the first ice.

13th ditto, latitude 74° 50', longitude 24° 35'; met with a border of ice.

14th ditto, latitude by observation 75° 44', longitude 26° 13'; came against some ice.

15th ditto, latitude 76° 13', longitude 25° 40'; saw Spitzbergen, the South Cape; bore East North East fourteen miles.

N. B. Drove about in the ice; made fast to a field.

25th ditto, in the morning saw the North Foreland, North East by East, latitude 79° 12', longitude 20° 40'.

26th ditto, latitude by observation 79° 10'.

27th ditto, against the ice.

28th ditto, passed through some ice.

29th ditto, got fast in the ice; saw two ships sailing pretty freely in the East North East.

N. B. in the ice till the

7th of June, got more room; beat to the Southward, and made fast to a field; saw land in

the East North East, distance fourteen or fifteen
miles ; supposed it the Quade Hoek, latitude
by observation 79° 58′ ; made fast to the ice
till the

11th June, at noon ; a violent storm, wind
South West, latitude by observation 80° 19′. In
the night, drove towards the coasts, for it blew
too hard to carry sail.

12th ditto, in the morning, laid fast in the
ice, the storm continued, and the ship so much
pressed by the ice, that we were obliged to un-
hang the rudder.

13th ditto, hard pressed by the ice, latitude
by observation 80° 29′. Remained pressed by
the ice till the

18th ditto, latitude by observation 80° 50′ ;
the ship not moveable.

19th ditto, latitude by observation 80° 57′ ;
the ice in great motion.

20th ditto, fast in the ice again, latitude by
observation 80° 58′ ; calm till the

24th ditto, began to blow a storm ; got some
room in the ice.

25th ditto, having got more room we advanced.

26th ditto, locked up again.

27th ditto, saw the land, namely, the Dorre Hoek, South by East half East, and the Vlakke Hoek, East South East ; lay beset till the

29th ditto, latitude by observation 80° 16'.

30th ditto, wind North East.

1st of July, saw water in the West South West, which we had not seen for many days. In the afternoon got more room.

2d ditto, worked our way through as much ice as we could, wind East North East, towards the evening North ; made fast to a field.

3d ditto, at noon, saw the land, being the Robbe Bay, bearing South West by West about one mile.

I have left out many little circumstances respecting the wind, tides, &c., as thinking the above sufficient for ascertaining the latitudes, and to show the method in which many of the Greenland Masters keep their Journals. That

year seems to have been favourable for getting
more to the North; for, notwithstanding
Mr. Breet met with so much ice, from the
latitude of 79° 30' to that of 80° 58', Captain
Jan Klaas Castricum, in the ship the Jonge Jan,
at that very time of the year, and nearly in the
same longitude, reached 81° 40', by the medium
of several observations with forestaffs, where he
fished with success, iu company with Witje
Jelles, who sailed from Hamburg, and found
but little ice. There were likewise two English
ships, who sailed so far to the North, that
Castricum lost sight of them from the mast
head, which two ships returned in something
more than two days, and the captains came
on board of Castricum*, and assured him, that
they had been to upwards of 83°, and could
have gone much farther, as they had no obstructions from ice, but finding no whales, they
returned. I spoke at the same time with other

* Captain Castricum neither asked their names, nor those
of their ships; all that he knew was, he said, if he remembered right, they sailed from England.

commanders, who, having been in sight of those
ships, confirmed Castricum's account.

Six of the oldest masters assured me (amongst
whom were John Walig, Klaas Keuken, and
J. Klaas Castricum), that they had known, from
1730 to 1742, an old English commander, whose
name was Krickrack*; it was his custom between
the fisheries, if not obstructed by ice, to sail to
the Northward ; and some of them affirm, that
when they have been at an anchor in Bran-
dewyns Bay, he once stayed away ten, and at
another time twenty days, before his return, and
they are very sure that he reported (and they
have reasons to believe him), that he had been
two degrees, and even more, North of the Seven
Islands.   All I could farther learn of this
Mr. Krickrack was, that in 1740 he was in the
only ship sent from England ; that for several
voyages he had the same ship's company ; that
in or about 1742 he had the command of a
transport, on board of which he lost his life

* From 1730 to 1740, most of the Masters of English
Ships, fitted out for the Greenland Trade, were Dutchmen.

by a musket ball : they were certain that he kept Journals, out of which they think much light might be obtained.

The greatest part of the Dutch commanders live at the Helder. Mr. Walig and others assured me, that the most Northern voyage then ever heard of, and on which they could with certainty depend, was that of Jacob Schol in 1700, who had been so far North, that on his return he sailed with a fresh gale of wind, due South, forty-eight hours and then fell in with the Seven Islands ; he consequently had been (reckoning that run at only four Dutch miles an hour, which they thought too little) in upwards of 84° North Latitude. As Mr. Schol was an inhabitant of the Helder, they told me that they would strive to procure me his papers from his heirs ; and, if I mistake not, they said that they had actually seen those papers in their younger days.

Finding that Mr. Van Keulen had put down (in his chart) the land discovered by Captain Gillis, mentioned in Mr. Walig's letter, I went

to him, to see on what foundation he had placed
that discovery; but as those papers could not
be found, I applied to Mr. Walig, who told me,
that Mr. Cornelius Gillis had been an inhabitant of the Helder; that Walig, together
with Mr. Keuken, Mr. Baske, and others, since
dead, had often examined Gillis's papers, maps,
&c., and found that he was an enterprising man,
and very accurate in his remarks and charts;
that his grandson had his Journals and other
Papers in his possession; and his grand-
daughter, who was married to an Officer of
Walig's Ship (who had formerly been a commander) had his charts, some of which that
officer generally took with him, in order to
correct them. I begged hard to have them, if
only for twenty-four hours; and next morning
Mr. Walig put into my hands the original
draughts of all the discoveries Mr. Gillis ever
made with regard to Spitzbergen, excepting
some particular drawings of bays and views of
land, with permission to keep them in my possession till Mr. Walig's return from Greenland;

copies of which are here annexed *, and Mr. Walig promised to procure me, if possible, all the papers of that old commander before he left the Texel, which I hope to receive in a few days, and shall not fail in sending over every thing I find material. Asking what particulars Mr. Walig and others remembered out of those papers, they gave the following short account. That Mr. Gillis passed more than a degree to the Northward of the Seven Islands, without any hindrance from ice: that he proceeded East for some leagues with an open sea, then bent his course South East, and afterwards South; saw in the latitude of 80°, to the East, very high land; run through the East Coast of the North East Land, and entered the Waygats Straits; came to an anchor in Lamber Bay, and took two whales, and from thence proceeded to the Texel. Mr. Baske gave also an account of his uncle's having, in company with three ships,

* These were copies of the draughts of the different coasts of Spitzbergen, of which Captain Gillis hath taken accurate surveys.

entered Waygats from the North, and advanced as far as the same bay, but found too much ice to get through, which the other three, being young commanders, made a trial of. The North Passage, however, on their return being shut, and it being the beginning of September, they made preparation to leave their ships, in order to get over land to Smeerenberg, but the ice luckily giving way, they got out to the Northward. Mr. Baske, who is a curious man, promised me, amongst other things, his thermometrical observations, which, by the conversation I had about them, I have reason to think will be accurate.

After having passed six mornings with a great number of our commanders quartered in different houses, I find, that scarcely a year had passed but some of them h 've been to 81° North, but rarely found the seas free from ice.

This is all the information I have been able to procure during my short stay at Amsterdam, which I would have prolonged, if a call to the Hague had not prevented me. I can only add, that waiting upon Mr. Boreel, that gentleman promised that he would order a search to be made for the Journals of those ships, which were formerly employed in protecting our Greenland Fisheries. I must, however, not forget to mention a particular that Mr. Van Keulen acquainted me with. He had, at his house, last summer, a conversation with a Russian, who had passed the winter last year in Spitzbergen, and gave him the following account. That being in the utmost distress, for want of eatables, on the North Coast, he made a trial to get with his boat towards the middle of the island, by means of the Bay of Wyde Bay in Gillis's Map, into which he proceeded, till, to his great surprise, he fell into Wybe Jansz's Bay, and so came out to the South of Spitzbergen; but he had taken no notice of the depths of water. Being questioned as to that particular, he said he was very sure that he did not pass through the Waygats.

In all my conversation with our Greenland

commanders, I never failed to ask which course
they would take to reach high Northern Latitudes ; the result was, that they would never
seek it to the Westward of Spitzbergen, but run
out to the North, from the West Coast of Nova
Zembla ; Mr. Baske's reasons and those of
other commanders were,

1st, That all the Western coast of the Northern countries were, for the most part, free
from ice, occasioned from the winds and tides
chiefly coming from the East, which experience proves,

2d, That the ice comes originally from the
Tartarian Rivers ; for, that the sea never
freezes but where it is calm, and at the same
time a great quantity of snow falls,

3d, That near the Seven Islands navigators
often meet with a great North East swell,
which proves, that at such time the sea, to a
considerable distance to the North East, is
not locked up by the ice.

4th, That the drift wood could not come to
the Northward of Spitzbergen, in case the

seas between the North of Asia and that
island were frozen ; whereas a great quantity
of that wood is drove on the North Coast of
Iceland, which is a demonstration that the
currents come from the North East.

5th, That in some of the trees the marks of the
axe were very plain, and the colour of the
wood so fresh, that they certainly had not
been six months in the sea.

6th, That some whole trees appeared with buds
thereon, which they think could not have
remained so fresh, if the trees had been a
year in the salt water.

7th, That the East of Greenland was now discovered to the latitude of $79\frac{1}{2}°$, that it probably extended farther to the North North
East, which they look upon to be cause
of the stoppage of ice between that coast
and Spitzbergen, and the reason why they
never find a North West or Northerly
swell.

8th, That generally all ships, which had once
got to the North as far as $82°$, met with little

or no obstructions from the ice; and more arguments to the same purpose. There were some, however, would rather make the trial between Spitzbergen and the land discovered by Mr. Gillis.

N. B. They knew nothing of the Papers read before the Royal Society.

TO ROD. VALLTRAVERS, ESQ. &c.

SIR,

PROFESSOR Allamand, being very desirous that the inclosed might be sent to you as soon as possible, has obliged me to draw up with haste the above account of the informations I received at Amsterdam. In reading it over and comparing it with my notes, I find no fault as to the facts related, whatever there may be in the manner in which it is drawn up; in case the whole or any part of it should be thought worth publishing, I hope you will be so good as to have it corrected *.

* This hath been done in some trifling particulars, relative merely to the stile, as Captain May is not a native of England.

M

I could have made it more circumstantial, as my notes are very full, in particular with regard to the reasons our commanders gave for not making the trial to the West of Spitzbergen, &c.

I am informed, that Mr. De Bougainville intends to go by the way of Nova Zembla*.

I am, with profound respect,

Sir,

Your most obedient humble Servant,

WILLIAM MAY.

Leyden,
April 11th, 1775.

* This voyage of discovery, however, did not take place.

THUS do the Dutch Seamen, employed in the Greenland Fishery, agree with our own countrymen, in never having so much as heard of a perpetual barrier of fixed ice, to the Northward of Spitzbergen, in 80½°*, which indeed is one of their most common latitudes for catching whales, whilst all of them suppose the sea to be generally open in those parts, and many of them proceed several degrees beyond it.

I shall only add, that in my former pamphlet †, I have mentioned a fact or two I had reason to expect from the Rev. Mr. Tooke, Chaplain to the factory at Petersburgh, which he conceived would strongly prove that the sea is open to the Pole, and which I have since received in a letter from him dated the 26th of May last.

Mr. Tooke hath been assured by several

* One of them indeed says, that the ice frequently *packs* in that latitude, which he supposes to arise from the meeting of two currents.

† Page 49, note.

persons, who have passed the winter at Kola in Lapland, that in the severest weather, whenever a Northerly wind blows, the cold diminishes instantly, and that, if it continues, it always brings on a thaw as long as it lasts.

He hath also been informed by the same authority, that the seamen, who go out from Kola upon the whale and morse fisheries early in March (for the sea never freezes there), throw off their winter garments as soon as they are from fifty to one hundred wersts * from land, and continue without them all the time they are upon the fishery, during which they experience no inconvenience from the cold, but that, on their return (at the end of May), as they approach land, the cold increases to such a severity, that they suffer greatly from it.

This account agrees with that of Barentz, whilst he wintered in Nova Zembla †, and that of the Russians in Maloy Brun: the North

* Three wersts make two miles.

† See Thoughts on the Probability, &c., of reaching the North Pole.

wind cannot therefore, during the coldest seasons of the year, be supposed to blow over ten degrees of ice.

Governor Ellis indeed, whose zeal in prosecuting the attempt of discovering the North West passage through Hudson's Bay is so well known, hath suggested to me an argument, which seems to prove the absolute impossibility of a perpetual barrier of ice from $80\frac{1}{2}°$ to the Pole.

If such a tract hath existed for centuries, the increase, in point of height, must be amazing in a course of years, by the snow, which falls during the winter, being changed into ice, and which must have formed consequently a mountain perhaps equal to the Peak of Teneriffe*. Now the ice, which sometimes *packs* to the Northward of Spitzbergen, is said commonly not to exceed two yards in height.

D. B————.

* Mr. De Luc observes also that the ice upon the Glacieres is always increasing. — See his interesting observations on those mountains of Switzerland.

OBSERVATIONS

ON THE

FLOATING ICE,

WHICH IS FOUND IN

HIGH NORTHERN AND SOUTHERN LATITUDES.

———◆———

SINCE the return of the King's ships from
voyages of discovery, both in high Northern
and Southern Latitudes, I have found that it
hath been a disputed point, whether the ice
which they have met with was formed chiefly
from the salt or fresh water. I should rather
conceive that this doubt must have arisen from
what is mentioned by the great Mr. Boyle, in
his experiments on heat and cold; or from an
observation of M. Adanson, at the end of his
voyage from Senegal, because from the quantity

of ice merely (at least to the Northward) the
early navigators never conceived that it was
produced from sea water.

In full proof of this, not to state the opinion
of several others on the same head, I shall content myself with citing that of Sir Martin
Frobisher, who is well known to have made
three successive voyages to Greenland, with a
farther intent of discovering the North West
Passage from Europe to the Pacific Ocean.
In the second voyage of this celebrated navigator, he observes:—

" We found none of these islands of ice salt
in taste, whereby it appears that they were not
of the ocean water congealed, which is always
salt, but of some standing or little moving
lakes ; the main sea freezes not, and therefore
there is no *Mare Glaciale.*"

In his third voyage he most anxiously repeats
this same opinion, and in still stronger terms,
so that what he hath thus laid down was not
an occasional observation merely, but what he
had much reflected upon, and found to be con-

firmed by his experience in those Northern Seas *.

This opinion of Sir Martin Frobisher's seems not to have been disputed by any one, till the time of Mr. Boyle, who observes, that there are several in Amsterdam, who used to thaw the ice of sea water for brewing, and then cites Bartholinus *De Nivis usu*. " *De glacie ex aquâ marinâ, certum est si resolvatur, salsum saporem deposuisse, quod non ita pridem expertus est Clarissimus* FINKIUS *in glaciei frustris, ex portu nostro allatis*†."

I shall not now criticise either what falls from Mr. Boyle himself or from Bartholinus, though it is very clear that the ice alluded to by both must have probably been formed from fresh water, either in the rivers, or lakes which empty themselves into the Zuyder Sea, because

---

* See Hakluyt, vol. ii, p. 62 and 67. In 1776, Mr. Marshall, Captain of a Greenland Ship, was so good as to bring me a bottle of water, which was melted from ice found floating in the Spitzbergen seas, and which had not the least saline taste.

† Boyle's Works, vol. ii, p. 264, folio.

I shall hereafter contradict the assertion of Bartholinus, by the actual experiment, which I have tried myself during the late hard frost.

To do justice indeed to Mr. Boyle, he afterwards, upon more mature consideration, shows it to be his opinion, agreeable to that of Sir Martin Frobisher, that the fresh water obtained from ice floating in the sea proves it could not have been formed from the ocean, " because the main sea is seldom or ever frozen *."

The next author, who supposes that congealed sea water is by this process rendered sweet to the taste, is M. Adanson, who informs us, that, upon his return from Senegal in 1748, he carried two bottles of sea water, taken up on the Coast of Africa, from Brest to Paris, which, during an intense frost, was so frozen as to burst the bottles, and the contents afterwards became palatable †.

To this fact I shortly answer, either that

* Boyle's Works, vol. ii, p. 302.

† Voyage au Senegal, p. 190.

the bottles were changed, or otherwise that
M. Adanson does not mention the circumstance by which the taste of the sea water
was thus altered upon its being dissolved.
Mr. Nairne hath been much more accurate in
stating his experiments with regard to the
freezing sea water, in a paper read before the
Royal Society on the 2d of February, 1776, as
he mentions, that, in order to clear the ice from
any brine, which might adhere to it, he washed
it in a pail of pump water for a quarter of an
hour, after which he informs the Society, that
to his palate it was perfectly free from any taste
of salt.

This is most undoubtedly the fact, but
Mr. Nairne does not seem to be aware from
what circumstance the ice thus melted had
become fresh water * ; and indeed I must admit,

---

* As Mr. Nairne, in his Letter to Sir John Pringle, says,
that one of his great reasons for trying these experiments
was to determine whether the ice, which floats in the Northern Seas, is formed from the salt water or not, he therefore
should have thawed the ice precisely under the same cir-

that upon the first experiment which I made
with regard to freezing sea water, I deduced
the same inference that he hath done, having
washed it in fresh water for the same reason
that he did, *viz.* to get rid of the brine which
might adhere to the surface of the ice.

To determine, therefore, whence this fresh-
ness in the thawed ice might arise, I placed

cumstances with the sea water adhering, as the navigators
take it up. The truth is, that, if the piece of ice formed
from sea water is at all large, the adhering salt water can
scarcely affect the taste at all; and I have melted the central parts of a pretty large mass, which became very salt
after dissolution, though entirely detached from the sea
water in which it had been frozen. " In the severe frost
last January (*viz.* 1775), some salt water, being set abroad,
froze into an ice, which was not solid but *porous*, the hollows
being filled with the saltest part of the water, for the ice
when *drained* was quite fresh. The salt water being again
set abroad, froze as before, what remained still unfrozen
was now become exceeding salt, but the ice drained and
dissolved was little if at all brackish; by this experiment,
if another time more fully repeated, it may be found to what
degree the saltness of water may be increased, by continuing to freeze away the fresh water."—Mr. Barker in Phil.
Trans. vol. lxvi, p. ii, 1776, p. 373.

a large piece of what remained frozen (without being washed at all in pump water) to be dissolved before the fire, which tasted very salt, as one might naturally suppose.

The weather continuing to be very severe, I froze more sea water, repeating the experiment of freshening it or not, by leaving or not leaving it in pump water, which always turned out uniformly to be the same; and the reason of which is the following.

When sea water is frozen, it does not form ice similar to that from fresh water, being by no means so solid or transparent, as it consists of thin laminæ or plates, between which the brine is deposited, and if the ice is accurately examined, the small portions of brine between the plates may be easily distinguished. If this brine therefore is removed, the laminæ of ice when dissolved become sweet to the taste, but, if thawed together with the brine intercepted between the laminæ, the taste is salt, nor can the ice be considerably divested of the brine, by merely leaving it to drain.

Having satisfied myself thus far from the freezing sea water by the natural cold, and under the common circumstances of exposing it to the air in small china cups, I applied to Dr. Higgins to prosecute these trials with his more ample apparatus, and knowledge of chemistry; who was immediately so good as to suggest and try the following experiments, which will throw farther light upon this subject*.

" JANUARY 2d†, 1776. A gallon, Winchester measure, of sea water, which I had fresh imported from Mr. Owen in Fleet Street, was placed in a shallow dish of Welsh ware, glazed

---

* It would be great injustice to Mr. Lomonosoff, a Swedish chemist, not to mention that he seems to have tried experiments similar to those which I have made myself, and found the result to be as I have stated it. *Collection Académique*, tom. xi, p. 5, *et seq.* 4to, Paris, 1772.—See also the Probability of reaching the North Pole discussed.

† Mr. Nairne began his experiments at the latter end of this month.

yellow; the depth of the water was three inches and a half in this shallow dish, which I marked A, and placed on a brick wall eight feet high above the ground behind my house. This wall on the Eastern side faces the gardens belonging to five or six houses in the same street with mine; and on the Western side of it is the area between my house and the elaboratory; and Westward of my area is the garden of Messrs. Wedgwood and Bentley, which I believe is forty feet wide, bounded on the West by high buildings.

At the same time I placed another gallon of the same sea water in a glass body. The column of water in this vessel was about thirteen inches high, about six inches diameter at the base, and about three inches at the mouth of the vessel. I placed this body with the sea water close by the vessel marked A; so that both were equally distant from the adjoining houses; and after marking the glass body B, I covered the vessels A and B with glass basons in such a manner, that the air might commu-

nicate with the surface of the water, but rain or
snow might be excluded.

" A Thermometer was placed between these
vessels.

" From the 2d to the 7th of January, the
mercury in the thermometer stood, at various
times, as low as 31° of Fahrenheit; and Thames
water, in shallow wooden vessels, placed on the
ground, near the wall above mentioned, was
often frozen to the thickness of a crown piece.
But an earthen oil jar containing twenty gallons of Thames water, and a like jar containing
twenty gallons of distilled water, and each
covered with a pewter dish, preserved the water
contained in them from freezing during this
interval.

" About the 7th of January, the mercury
in the course of twenty four hours did not
rise above 31°, but sometimes sunk to 30°.
Ice was formed in the vessel marked A; but
none in the vessel marked B. Ice was at the
same time formed in the great jars containing
Thames water and distilled water; and to a

thickness much greater in the Thames water than in the water distilled. The ice obtained from the vessel A was all formed on the surface of the water; and consisted of thin laminæ adhering to each other weakly, and intercepting in their interstices a small portion of water, which was saline to the taste. This ice, beaten gently with a glass pestle to divide the laminæ, then drained, and then washed in distilled water, tasted like the ice of fresh water; and being placed in a glass funnel before a culinary fire, so that the water might drain off as soon as formed, it dissolved in half an hour, and not in less time, although the thermometer placed at the same distance close to the funnel rose to a hundred and sixty; and the side of the funnel next to the fire was hot to the like degree, as nearly as could be ascertained by the touch. The water of the ice thus melted was fresh and palatable, and measured half a pint.

" From the 9th of January to the 11th inclusive, the mercury rose some days to forty, and during three or four hours on other days it sunk and remained at thirty, and sometimes for an hour or less it sunk to twenty-nine. But it did not remain at thirty during any of these days for more than four or five hours, unless at the hours of rest, when no observation was made. During this period, a thin coat of ice, like the former, was produced on the water in the shallow vessel A; but no ice was formed in the vessel B.

" January 12, the thermometer pointed for several hours between thirty-one at the highest, and twenty-nine at the lowest. A thick crust of ice, of the texture before described, was formed in the vessel A. This ice broken, washed, and dissolved, became fresh water, measuring a pint or more. This quantity of ice, placed in a funnel before a fire, in the circumstances already described, was not all dissolved in an hour and ten minutes. No ice was formed in the vessel B *.

" January the 13th at night, and 14th in

* " The foregoing observations were committed to writing on the days when they were respectively made, but the day of the month was not then accurately noted. It

the morning, the thermometer sunk for some
hours below twenty-seven, and did not rise
during sixteen hours above twenty-eight. The
water in the vessel A, remaining after the foregoing congelations, was frozen to the thickness
of a quarter of an inch in the centre, and
three quarters of an inch in the circumference;
but no ice was formed at any greater depth in
the water. This ice, like the former, was laminated, and when bruised and washed, it formed
fresh water to the quantity of three pints.

" On the same day, *viz.* 14th of January, in
the morning, the thermometer pointing below
twenty-seven, the Thames water in the great jar
was frozen to the thickness of three or four
inches, if not more, contiguous to the jar and
the surface. The distilled Thames water in the
other jar was frozen to the thickness of two
inches, or thereabouts, and contiguous to the
jar and surface of the water; and the sea water

may therefore be found that I have placed some of the
foregoing temperatures a day before or after that on
which they were observed."

in the glass body marked B was for the first
time frozen. On the surface, and in the centre
of this surface, the ice was half an inch thick ;
at the circumference it was an inch thick ; and
from the circumference and surface the ice
formed contiguous to the glass, in such a manner, that the crust was an inch thick near the
glass and surface ; but, as it proceeded downwards towards the wider part of the glass, it
tapered to an edge, terminating within an inch
of the bottom of the vessel.

" Thus all the ice was formed on the surface
and contiguous to the glass, and was thickest
where the vessel was narrowest ; that is, the
quantity of ice was inversely as the diameter of
the vessel. This ice resembled that obtained in
the shallow vessel in its laminated structure and
sponginess, and in its enveloping a portion of
the salt water, with this difference only, that the
laminæ shot vertically, and from the circumference inclining towards the centre, not directly,
but so as to form with the centre an angle of
about fifteen degrees. This ice, bruised and

washed, melted to a pint and a half of pleasant fresh water. The time and heat were nearly the same as I described above.

" Mr. Barrington at this and former periods observed, that the separation of the laminæ of the ice by bruising accelerated the effect produced by washing ; that is, the extrication of the intercepted brine.

" January the 19th at night, the mercury in the thermometer sunk to twenty-six. The sea water, remaining after the foregoing congelations in the flat dish marked A, was frozen so far, that only a pint remained fluid at the bottom. This ice was in all respects like the former portions. Bruised, washed, and melted, as on former occasions, it gave a quart of fresh water. At the same time, the water in B was frozen in the manner before described, but in a larger quantity, and some laminæ of ice shot close to the glass as far as the bottom of the vessel. This ice bruised and washed as formerly, and placed before the fire in a glass funnel, melted in a heat of a hundred and sixty, in an hour and a half, to one quart of fresh water.

" January the 20th, the mercury, which stood at twenty-seven in the morning, and fell to twenty-six towards twelve o'clock, fell in a few hours to twenty-four, and, before nine at night, fell to twenty-three. Only a thin coat of ice was formed on the water in A, which I did not disturb, expecting it to freeze deeper during the night. The water in the vessel B was frozen to some thickness at the surface, and contiguous to the sides of the glass body, but not at the bottom. Expecting a stronger congelation, I suffered this also to stand until the next morning, and consequently could not determine the quantity of ice formed in it, otherwise than by feeling near the surface, whereby I presumed the quantity of ice to be equal to that last obtained, and formed in the same manner.

" January the 21st in the morning, the thermometer pointed to twenty-eight. The thin crust of ice, observed on the preceding night, did not appear to be increased or diminished in the vessel marked A. The laminæ of this ice adhered so weakly, that the whole crust could not be raised without break ing This ice, bruised and well washed, dissolved to near half a pint of water, brackish to the taste. And the same day, in the morning, the ice in B was removed, bruised, and washed; it melted to a pint or more of fresh water.

" From the 21st to the 26th of January, the water in the vessel marked B was frozen twice, and the ice formed each time was bruised and washed, and melted to fresh water, both portions measuring one pint or more.

" From the 26th of January at sun set, to the 27th at eleven o'clock in the morning, the mercury in the thermometer stood, at the usual hours of observation, between twenty and eighteen. The water remaining after the foregoing congelations in B was frozen so far, that only half a pint remained fluid. The ice, bruised, washed, and dissolved, tasted a little brackish, and measured one pint and a half.

" On the 28th of January the mercury stood
in the morning and until four o'clock in the
afternoon between twenty-two and nineteen,
and before eleven o'clock at night it sunk to
seventeen. Very little ice was formed in the
vessel B; and what was formed very easily
crumbled or fell to small flakes in attempting to
take it out. I therefore suffered it to remain in
the liquor until the morning.

" On the 29th of January the mercury stood
between twenty and twenty-two until six o'clock;
and between twenty and nineteen, from six
until twelve at night. The quantity of ice,
formed on the preceding day, was not notably
augmented or diminished; bruised, washed, and
melted, it yielded two ounces of water, brackish
to the taste, in a greater degree than any of the
foregoing portions which were washed.

" On the 30th of January, finding that the
temperature of the preceding evening, of the
night, and of this day, which was between nineteen and twenty-one, had caused no notable
congelation in the small quantity of water re-

maining in B; finding also that the residue of
the water in A admitted of no farther congelation worth notice; and considering that the
slender laminæ of ice, lately formed in these
waters, melted to salt water, and consequently
that no farther congelation, capable of sepa-
rating the fresh water from the brine, even with
the assistance of washing, could take place;
I mixed the concentrated brine in A with that
in B, and found both scarcely measured a wine
pint; some small crystals were found in the
bottom of both vessels, which sunk in the brine,
and were to the taste sea salt. It is hence
evident that some sea salt is formed in crystals
by the concentration produced by cold acting
gradually, and causing congelation only on the
surface of the water, or not affecting that part
of it which is contiguous to the bottom of the
vessel.

" The quantity of these crystals of sea salt
was about two grains. I poured them together
with the water into a china plate, set in a sand
heat, and, by crystallization, obtained sea salt

and the other saline contents of sea water, in a dry form, near two ounces averdupois.

"Now, as this quantity of sea water (that is, two gallons), taken on our coast, generally yields about seven ounces of saline matters, it appears, that two-thirds or more of the sea salt, and bitter salts of sea water, are intercepted in the ice of the successive congelations, and are washed away by fresh water, applied as above mentioned, Hence we learn that sea water may be freshened by freezing, provided the brine enveloped between the laminæ of its ice be washed away. And in cold countries salt might be prepared from sea water at a very moderate expense ; for by freezing shallow ponds of this water, by turning the ice to drain off the brine, and when the brine is reduced to a twentieth part or less by evaporation, very little evaporation and fuel will be necessary towards the formation of the salt *. But all the salt of the sea water employed will not be ob-

* "Wallerius says, this art is practised in the Northern countries."

tained, because the greater part of it will be re-
tained between the laminæ of the ice, which
must be rejected; and the concentration by
freezing cannot be advantageously carried farther
than is above expressed, because at that degree
of concentration the cold, and the time necessary to cause farther congelations, must be very
considerable, as will the waste of salt likewise,
since the ice is then strongly saline.

"A small portion of the ice, taken at various
times from B since the 26th of January, was
not washed, but only left to drain in a funnel;
and each portion thus drained during five or six
days, being separately dissolved, tasted strongly
of salt, although the like ice, which was bruised
and washed, yielded fresh water. This proves
that washing removes the intercepted brine;
and that this brine does not separate by
draining.

"January the 20th, at eight o'clock in the
evening, the thermometer pointing at twenty
three, in the open air where the thermometer
stood, I mixed snow with smoking spirit of

nitre, and placed in the mixture a glass half
pint tumbler full of sea water ; and at the same
time placed the thermometer in the mixture.
In two minutes the mercury sunk out of the
tube quite into the globe. The scale extends
only twenty-five degrees below 0 of Fahrenheit ;
wherefore I could not determine how many degrees lower it would have sunk on a more extended scale. In five minutes, some slender
laminæ of ice began to shoot from the circumference of the water, and adhered to the glass.
The whole water was *not frozen in less than an
hour*, at which time the mercury in the thermometer rose to twenty degrees below 0.
Having another mixture of the same kind ready
made, I briskly removed the tumbler with the
ice it contained into the fresh mixture, which,
like the former, sunk the mercury into the
globe.

"The ice of sea water is more opaque than
that of fresh water, when both are naturally
congealed. For the elastic fluid in common
water forms bubbles only in the central parts

of the water last frozen; but the ice of sea
water consists of alternate parts of ice and
brine; the density of which being unequal, and
the matter of them being also dissimilar, light
cannot be freely transmitted, but is partly reflected and refracted, according to Sir Isaac
Newton's ideas of light.

" In the experiment last mentioned, the ice
was commonly opaque; and when it was exposed to the fresh frigorific mixture, it became
like a mass of snow compressed, having a snowy
whiteness and opacity, perfect near the surface,
but not perfect towards the bottom.

" The tumbler, with the ice it contained,
was kept in this last mentioned mixture an
hour, when the mercury denoted that no farther
degree of cold could be given by this mixture.
The tumbler was then placed in snow until the
next day, to preserve the ice for farther observation. Notwithstanding the extreme cold to
which it had been so long exposed, and the cold
medium in which it was placed, the ice was not
solid like that of fresh water, but, on the con-

trary, could easily be cut through the centre of
the mass with a knife. The ice tasted equally
of salt through the whole mass, in the same
manner as a like quantity of sea water.
Bruised briskly, washed as already described,
and melted, it yielded fresh water to the quantity of four-fifths of the water frozen ; wherefore in washing very little ice was dissolved,
whilst the salt water intercepted in the ice was
removed.

    " Mr. Barrington having observed that an
artificial freezing commences from the bottom
and sides of the mass of water placed as usual
in the frigorific mixture, but that natural freezing commences on the surface and proceeds
downwards ; and it occurring to me that the
specific gravity of incongelable brine is greater
than that of the congelable water; and, consequently, that this greater specific gravity favours
the separation of brine from the ice of sea
water, when the freezing commences on the
surface of sea water, and may be an impediment
to the separation of the incongelable brine from

the ice artificially formed in the sea water, when
the congelation proceeds from the bottom upwards; on these considerations it seemed that
the foregoing experiments indicate, that ice
formed in sea water cannot, when melted, become fresh water, unless it be washed in fresh
water; but do not fully prove, that ice formed
on the surface only, and proceeding slowly
downwards, in sea water, may not consist of
fresh water, and be freed from brine, by reason
of the specific gravity of brine and other un-
noticed circumstances. Therefore, on the 21st
of January, at two o'clock, when the mercury
stood in the open air at twenty-nine, I made
the following experiment, with a view to determine whether sea water, frozen artificially from
the surface downwards in the manner performed
by nature, would not yield ice of a solid texture
capable of melting to fresh water, without
washing, merely by draining; which must take
place in mountains of ice, if any are formed in
the Northern Sea: because, ice being specifi-
cally lighter than water, and the access of con-

gealed water being at the base, the portions
first frozen will be raised above the water by
succeeding portions frozen, and thus a mountain of ice may be raised, whose mass and height
above water will be to the massive base immersed in water, inversely as the specific gravity
of ice is to that of water.

" I placed therefore a gallon of sea water in
a glazed earthen vessel, whose diameter was
one third greater than the depth of the water.
In this water I slung a thin glass bason, cut
from a bolt head, capable of containing near
two quarts of water, in such manner that it
might be immersed two inches deep in the sea
water. The vessel containing the sea water
was surrounded with snow. I then filled the
bason, which was suspended in the sea water,
with snow pressed down with a glass pestle,
and poured into the snow the usual quantity of
strong nitrous acid.

" In fifteen minutes some crystals of ice
were formed on the interior glass bason, in the
part where it was contiguous to the surface of

the sea water. In three hours the whole
bottom of the bason, containing the frigorific
mixture, was coated with ice, the thickness of
which was half an inch or less at the bottom of
the bason, increasing to three-fourths of an inch
at the part which corresponded with the surface
of the water.

" I easily separated it entire from the bason,
found it somewhat firmer in its aggregation
than the ice slowly formed by natural freezing,
and not composed of laminæ like this latter,
but similar in texture to the salt water frozen
by artificial cold applied in the usual manner.
I placed it on a heap of snow, where it remained to drain upwards of six hours, but still
was wet to the touch on the surface, and in the
fresh surfaces of the fractured parts. I then
placed a part of it in a glass funnel before the
fire to melt, and found the water strongly
saline to the taste, but not near so saline as
equal parts of sea and river water mixed.

" Another portion of this ice, which was
wrapped up in filtering paper, and left to drain

on a heap of dry snow during four days, when melted, was saline to the taste, and not sensibly different from that which had drained only six or seven hours. Whence it appeared, that ice formed in the sea water, in circumstances similar to those which attend natural congelation, is, nevertheless, saline to the taste.

" The several portions of water obtained in the foregoing experiments, from the washed ice of the sea water in A and B, being preserved in glass stopper bottles, were not examined. Although they were fresh to the taste,. it appeared by the quantity of *luna cornea,* which they all formed with saturated nitrous solution of silver, that they were strongly impregnated with marine salt, comparatively with Thames and New River water, examined in the like manner.

" Mr. Barrington, observing that salt in water is an impediment to the congelation of that water, presumed, that salt in water would accelerate the thawing of ice immersed in it; and that in equal temperatures ice would be thawed in sea water sooner than in fresh water. I therefore made the following experiment.

" January the 20th, when the thermometer pointed to twenty three, about nine o'clock at night, I placed five ounces and half a drachm, avoirdupois, of Thames water in a half pint glass tumbler; and the like quantity of the same water distilled in another half pint glass tumbler of equal figure and capacity with the foregoing. The tumblers were placed on the wall formerly described, and left there covered with glass until eleven o'clock next morning.

" In the morning at eleven o'clock, the thermometer pointed to twenty-eight. The water in both tumblers was frozen quite through, and formed masses of ice, transparent as crystal in every part, except the centre, and near the bottom, which parts were rendered opaque to the thickness of half an inch, by a number of air bubbles locked up in the ice. The distilled water had been kept several days in the jar above described, whose mouth was only covered with an inverted pewter dish.

" Into a glass tumbler, capable of holding a
Winchester pint or more, I put a wine pint of
Thames water; and into another tumbler of
the same figure and capacity, I poured a pint
of sea-water concentrated, by freezing one
fourth of it, the better to represent sea water
of the great oceans, which are not affected by
rivers so much as the sea water used in these
experiments must be, as it was taken up near
the North Foreland. The sea water was thus
concentrated for these farther reasons : first,
that the effect of salt in the water might be
more conspicuous during the thawing of the
ice ; and secondly, to prevent the first portions
of ice thawed from diluting the salt water to a
degree which never is found in the ocean. I
reduced the sea and the Thames water, contained in these tumblers, to the same temperature exactly, in the open air; then taking
hold of each by the summit of the glass above
the water, I carried them into my study, and
placed them on a carpet fifteen feet equally
distant from the fire, and three inches from the

wainscot of the wall opposite the fire, and
equally distant from a door on one side, and à
window, which extends within fourteen inches
of the floor, on the other. The tumblers, containing the frozen water, were immersed in a
large pan of hot water, close to each other, and
near the centre of the pan, the water rising to
the height of the ice in the tumblers; after a
few minutes the ice was thrown out, by in-
verting the glasses on clean paper. The two
pieces of ice were equal in size,- figure, and
weight; the weight of each being five ounces
avoirdupois.

"The moment before the ice was taken out
of the tumblers, I found the temperature of the
sea and fresh water, placed as above-mentioned,
to be equal, and exactly thirty-four; the temperature of the air in that part of the room
being forty six. I plunged the pieces of ice
immediately, one in the sea water, the other in
the fresh water. It was at this instant two
o'clock in the afternoon. In ten minutes the
temperature of the sea water was thirty-two,

that of the fresh water was thirty-three and a half. In half an hour the sea water raised the mercury to thirty-three, the fresh water raised it to thirty-four and a half.

" At this instant, *viz.* half an hour past two o'clock, I took both the pieces of ice at the same time, weighed them briskly, and replaced them in their respective vessels at the same instant. Of the ice placed in the sea water, half an ounce was dissolved ; of the ice placed in the fresh water, only four drachms and a half were dissolved.

" From half an hour past two o'clock until six I frequently changed the position of the tumblers, making one take the place of the other. At six, the temperature of the sea water was thirty-six, that of the fresh water was thirty seven and a half. In the manner already mentioned, the ice was at this time weighed and replaced. Of the ice in sea water three ounces and four drachms were dissolved ; of that in fresh water, only two ounces and eight drachms.

" It is observable, that the sea water was
a degree and a half colder, ever since the immersion of the ice, than the fresh water, acted
on by the like mass of ice, and placed in the
like circumstances; and nevertheless the ice
was dissolved much quicker in the colder sea
water. The quicker solution of the ice in sea
water was evidently the cause of the greater
degree of cold preserved in it during four hours,
and it already appeared, that salt water is a
more powerful solvent of ice than fresh water
in the like temperature. And, agreeable to
Mr. Barrington's suggestion, the matter which
impedes the congelation of water must of course
facilitate the thawing of ice. The nitrous acid
furnishes us with another striking instance to
this effect; for no cold can be produced to
freeze the water in it; and a red hot ladle
cannot thaw ice placed in it, so quickly as ice is
thawed by nitrous acid.

" At ten o'clock, or in eight hours after the
pieces of ice were first placed in the sea and
Thames water, the temperature of the sea water

was thirty-nine, that of the Thames water only thirty-eight. At this time, of the ice in sea water four ounces eight drachms were dissolved; of the ice in Thames water, four ounces only were dissolved. The sea water being at this period warmer than the Thames water, corresponds with the small portion of ice remaining in it, compared with that remaining in the fresh water. The temperature of the room in the place where the tumblers stood, being, by reason of the fire kept constantly in it, forty-four or forty-five, for the last six hours.

" In twelve hours, or at two o'clock in the morning, the temperature of the room near the vessels of water being nearly the same as formerly described, the temperature of the sea water was forty, the temperature of the fresh water was thirty-nine. Four ounces fifteen drachms of the ice in salt water were dissolved, only one drachm remaining; four ounces ten drachms of the ice in fresh water were dissolved, only six drachms remaining.

"At the end of the thirteenth hour, after the immersion of the masses of ice in the fresh and in the salt water, that is, at three in the morning, the temperature of the room was forty-five near the place where the tumblers stood. The temperature of the open air was thirty-one. The ice in the sea water was melted. The quantity of ice remaining in the fresh water was one drachm, which, in fifteen minutes more, was entirely melted.

" At this period, when the ice in the fresh water was melted, that is, a quarter of an hour past three, the mercury stood at forty in the fresh water, in the salt water it stood at forty-one. In a quarter of an hour after this, the mercury stood at forty-two in the salt water, and at forty-one in the fresh water. In a quarter of an hour more, the temperature remained unalterable in the salt and fresh water, although the temperature of the air between and near the vessels was forty-five, and the vessel on the right was placed on the left, and replaced several times. And both vessels were at all times equidistant from the wainscot, which was perfectly close, as were the boards of the floor also.

" In a quarter of an hour more, the temperature of the air near and between the tumblers remained forty-five ; the temperature of the fresh water was scarcely forty-two ; the temperature of the salt water was forty-two and a half.

" In a quarter of an hour more, the temperature of the air between the tumblers being forty-four and a half, the temperature of the salt water was forty-three ; the temperature of the fresh water was somewhat more than forty-two. It was now past four o'clock in the morning, on Monday the 22d of January. I went to bed, leaving the tumblers in the position described.

" It was observed, during the foregoing and other experiments, and it is visible, from the experiments related, that fire, in diffusing itself from warm bodies to contiguous cold bodies, proceeds slowly ; that cold bodies do not acquire the temperature of the warmer medium in which they are immersed so soon as is commonly imagined, but, on the contrary, require a considerable time for that purpose ; and this time is directly as the diameter of the cold body,

" It was inferred from these experiments, that a temperate body, like water, placed in a cold medium, as in air, cooled to thirty or thirty-one of Fahrenheit, requires many hours before it acquires the temperature of the surrounding medium, and before a congelation commences ; and that the time necessary for the commencement of the congelation is directly as the mass and shortest diameter of the water, and the progress of the congelation is inversely as the depth of the water.

" It was also observed, that as much of a given mass of water was frozen in five hours in a temperature of twelve degrees below the freezing point, as was frozen in one hour in a temperature fifty degrees below the freezing point ; and that long duration of the temperature between twenty and thirty-two is, to-

wards the congelation of water, equivalent to
intensity of cold, such as is marked 0, and
below 0, in Fahrenheit, but of short duration.

" It was moreover observed, that water in
thick jars covered was not frozen, when water
in open vessels was frozen ; that water included
in massive vessels of wood, or surrounded by
any matter except water, to some thickness,
preserved its temperature, and resisted congelation, longer than the like quantity of water
exposed to the cold air ; and that water in
thick vessels was not frozen so soon as a like
quantity of water in thin vessels of like matter,
figure, and capacity. It was thence inferred, that
fire does not so quickly pervade thick bodies
as it does thin bodies ; and that fire pervades
water more freely than it does solid bodies, and
sooner diffuses itself from water to air, than
from any other body containing water to air.

" Thence it followed, that in reasoning on
the phænomena of congelation, the masses of
water, the duration of cold temperature in the
atmosphere, and the masses of other matter

surrounding water, are to be considered. Deep
rivers and lakes do not freeze so soon as shallow
rivers and lakes. Large bodies of water are
never frozen in any temperature of short duration ; but shallow waters are often frozen in the
summer.

" It need not be presumed, that certain
lakes, which are never frozen, communicate
with subterranean fires, or hot mineral streams;
or that they are impregnated with matter which
impedes congelation : but it is rather to be
presumed, that as fire slowly pervades, enters, or
quits bodies, the time necessary for its diffusing
itself from deep lakes to the cold atmosphere is
greater than ever such temperature of the atmosphere continues without intermission below
the freezing point.

" By the like reasoning applied to masses
of earth and other matter, which are not so
quickly pervaded by fire as water is, we can
conceive why deep wells and springs at or near
their issuing from the earth are not frozen in
this climate, even when navigable rivers are ice

bound. We also understand why the main
pipes, buried in our streets, retain the water
fluid, when the pipes leading from these to the
houses, and crossing the area of each house, are
choked with ice; and why hay bands twisted
round these small pipes prevent the freezing, &c.

"On these grounds it is presumed, that no
considerable congelation ever takes place in the
sea, because this is the greatest and deepest mass
of water we know of; because it is always in
motion, and communicates with the water of
temperate climates; because sea water is not so
easily frozen as fresh water; because the ice
found in the sea is solid, and in transparency
not different from the ice of fresh water;
and, lastly, because this floating ice, which is
met with by navigators, both in high Northern
and Southern Latitudes, when melted, is palatable to the taste; whereas the ice formed from
sea water is very saline, if it be thawed without
having been washed in fresh water.

"It is also presumed, that in the deep

Northern seas the water near the surface will be found warmer than that near the bottom at the approach of summer; and will be found colder near the surface than at the bottom in the first month of the cold season, for the reasons already expressed : and in like manner, that, during the first six or eight hours of a frost in England, the water in any deep lake will be found colder near the surface than at the bottom, but that the water at the bottom will be found colder than that near the surface in twenty-four hours after a thaw, provided the air be temperate, or nearly so."

It having been proved, from what hath been already urged, as well as by the preceding experiments of Dr. Higgins, that the floating ice, which is observed both in high Southern and Northern Latitudes, cannot be probably formed from sea water, it may be thought incumbent upon me to show how such quantities can be supplied from springs, rain, or frozen snow.

The rivers, which are always found at cer-

tain intervals in any large tract of land, undoubtedly supply considerable part of such ice ;
but there are not wanting other sources from
which these floating masses may be produced.

The larger and higher ice islands* I conceive to be chiefly formed on shore, after which
they are undermined by the rills and melted
snow, during the summer, of which we have an
accurate account in the late voyage towards the
North Pole†.

* Mr. Whales observes, that in the islands of ice, near
Georgia Australis and Sandwich Land, there are strata of
dirty *ice,* which irrefragably proves their having been
formed on the land. — Remarks on Dr. Forster's Account,
&c. 8vo. London, 1778, p. 106.

With regard to the formation of ice islands, see likewise
Captain Cook's Voyage, vol. ii, p. 213 and 240; who conceives them to arise from congealed snow and sleet in the
vallies.   Captain Cook also supposes, that the ice cliffs, at
the end of these vallies, often project a great way into the
sea, when they are sheltered from the violence of the wind,
p. 242.

† " Large pieces frequently break off from the ice bergs,
and fall with great noise into the water : we observed
one piece which had floated out into the bay, and grounded
in twenty-four fathoms; it was fifty feet high above the

Others, which happen to have projected

surface of the water, and of the same beautiful colour as the ice berg." p. 70.

I have likewise been favoured with the following account of ice islands on the coast of Labrador, from Lieutenant John Cartwright, of the Royal Navy, to whom I have not only this obligation.—See the Probability of reaching the North Pole, p. 8.

"Dear Sir,   "*Thursday, Feb.* 28, 1776.

" In conformity with my promise of yesterday, I now send you, as nearly as I can recollect, my brother's account (who hath resided four years on the Labrador Coast) of the formation of those great masses of frozen snow, seen annually in very great numbers on the Northern Coasts of America, and by mariners usually called *Islands of Ice.*

" Along the Coast of Labrador, the sea, in winter, is frozen to a great distance from the land. The North West is the prevailing and coldest wind. The snow, carried by this or any other Westerly Winds over the cliffs of the Coast, falls becalmed upon the ice at the foot of the said cliffs, drifting up to the very tops of them, although many of them are not inferior to that of Dover, or those about Lulworth. The current of the strong Western Winds, having passed these precipices, takes its course downwards into the undisturbed air below ; but it is not until it arrives at some distance from the land, that it can be felt on the surface of the sea. Having the frozen surface of the sea for a base, and the precipice for a

over the sea, may have had their foundations so

perpendicular, an hypothenuse is made by the descending
direction of the wind.   The enclosed triangle, be the cliffs
ever so high, will be filled with snow ; because the tops of
the adjoining hills, being quite naked, are entirely swept
clear of snow by the violence of the storms, and what would
otherwise have lain there is carried to the leeward of the
hills, and under the shelter of the cliffs, where it is deposited
in infinitely greater quantities than it would fall in without
such a cause.   The hypothenuse of such triangle is frequently of such a slope as that a man may walk up or down
without difficulty.   By frequent thaws, and the occasional
fall of moisture interrupting the frost, during the first parts
of the winter, the snow will, in some small degree, dissolve,
by which means it only acquires a greater hardness when the
frost returns ; and during the course of that rigorous season
it generally becomes a very compact body of snow ice.
In the spring of the year the icy base gives way, and
its burden plunges into the sea, sometimes entire, sometimes in many fragments.   As the depth of water in
many parts is forty, fifty, one hundred fathoms, and upwards, close to the shore, these bodies of ice, vast as is
their bulk, will frequently float without any diminution
of their contents, although the very large ones do often
take the ground, and sometimes are not sufficiently reduced by either the penetration of the sea and the rain
water, or of a whole summer's sun, to get at liberty
again before another winter.

    " The above relation, which my brother gives from his

sapped by the waves during a storm *, as to have lost their support; whilst others again may have been reft from the mass to which they before adhered by the expansive power of the frost †.

Great part of the field, or lower ice, I take to be formed by the snow falling on the sands left bare for six hours (from half ebb to half

own observation, in North Latitude 52° 15′, accounts very naturally and easily for the formation of that surprising number of the vast pieces of ice which is annually seen on the Labrador Coast, and considerably to the Southward.

" JOHN CARTWRIGHT."

* " The sea has washed underneath the ice cliffs, as high as the Kentish Forelands, and the arches overhanging support mountains of snow, which have lain since the creation."
—Wood's Voyage, p. 20.

" Cuncta gelu, canaque æternum grandine tecta,
    Atque ævi glaciem cohibent, riget ardua montis
    Ætherii facies, surgentique obvia Phœbo,
    Duratas nescit flammis mollire pruinas."
                    Silius Italicus, lib. iii, l. 480.

† " The rocks along the coast burst with a report equal to that of artillery, and the splinters are thrown to an amazing distance." Mr. Wales, in Philosophical Transactions, vol. lx, p. 125.

flood), which immediately dissolves upon touching the sands, and, before the tide returns, becomes solid ice; part of these pieces are by the wind, or tide, again returned to the same sands, where they again meet with another store of ice, formed during another six hours, which, in the course of a winter, must, by packing, accumulate to immense masses. That this is not mere conjecture, but the fact, I appeal to Captain James's account of what he himself was witness of whilst he wintered at Charlton Island, in Hudson's Bay[*].

Now, if we examine a globe, we shall find, that from sixty to seventy degrees of Northern latitude more than half its circumference is land, which is open to a Northern Sea, from which large tract of coast much greater quantities of floating ice may be derived than have ever been

---

[*] For Captain James's account, see Boyle, vol. ii; as also Harris, vol. ii, p. 420; where it is considerably abridged, and differs in some few circumstances. It is stated, however, that in a few hours the snow thus frozen will be five or six feet thick.

met with by navigators, without being obliged to suppose that any part of it is formed from sea water.

But it may be said, that our late enterprising navigators to the Southward have also met with as great a quantity of ice in the opposite hemisphere, without scarcely discovering any land.

To this I answer, that their circumnavigation was, at a medium, about 57° of Southern Latitude, though they made pushes greatly to the Southward in three points, and in one of these to 71° 10′. In the other instances, as far as 67° and 67° 30′.

There is consequently a very large space in which there may be many a frozen region, which they have not had any opportunity of discovering. If, for example, a navigator from the Southern was sent upon discoveries to the Northern hemisphere, and Europe, as well as Asia and North America, having been sunk by earthquakes, was to report that he had circumnavigated at 55° North Latitude at a medium; made pushes even to 71° in different directions, without seeing any continent; and that therefore there was no land to the North of 55°; his countrymen would be much deceived by such report, because Denmark, Norway, Sweden, Muscovy, Tartarian Asia, and part of North America, continued in their present situation.

Besides, however, the ice which may come from *Tierra del Fuego*, Captain Cook hath discovered two frozen islands between Cape Horn and that of Good Hope, which were covered with ice and snow*. The first of these,

* Hence whatever land is discovered to the South of this latitude must produce ice. There is also a large tract of land, named in some maps the *Gulph of St. Sebástian*, which is not far distant from *Georgia Australis*, and which possibly may have escaped Captain Cook. This great navigator also conceives, that the ice floats from 70° South, and is detached by accidents from land lying to the South of that parallel, as the currents in the Antarctic Seas always set to the North. — Cook's Voyage, vol. i, p. 268.

Captain Furneaux in 1744, passed between Georgia Australis and Sandwich Land (rather supposed a continent), without seeing either of these new discoveries, though the

situate in 54°, is called *Georgia Australis*; and the second, *Sandwich Land*, in 59°, which appeared so large, to some eyes, that it was conceived to be part of a continent *.

It is believed also, that no ship hath been beyond 48° to the Southward of New Zealand; and from the coldness of the most Southern of these large islands, I cannot but suspect that there is a considerable tract of land between it and the Pole.

Having thus endeavoured to account how the floating ice which is met with may be supposed to be formed from snow or fresh water;

mountains on both are remarkably high, particularly those in Sandwich Land, one of which, by several, was considered to equal Teneriffe.

Captain Furneaux could not have been well more than two degrees from either of these countries. — See his Track in the lately published Map.

* See Captain Cook's Voyage, vol. ii, p. 230; where he supposes land near the South Pole, chiefly opposite to the Southern Atlantic, and Indian Oceans, as on those meridians ice is found as far North as 48°. It is in this tract of Southern Land that Cook supposes the ice to be chiefly formed, which is met with in the Southern Oceans. — Ibid.

I cannot but risk another conjecture, that the time of the year at which attempts are commonly made to make discoveries towards the two Poles (though favourable in many other circumstances *) is probably the season when the greatest quantity of floating ice will be observed.

This seems to follow as a necessary consequence from the push being never made before Midsummer, and often a month later, which is precisely the time when the ice begins to break up in the fresh water rivers, &c.

I have accordingly minuted down, from several voyages into high Northern Latitudes, the day on which navigators first mention seeing the floating ice.

The result of which is as follows :—

Sir Martin Frobisher on the 23d of June. —Hackluyt, vol ii, p. 77.

---

* *Viz.* The nights being shorter, and the rigging not being so subject to be frozen.

Davis in his first voyage, July 19th, In his third, July 2d.—Ibid. p. 99.

Pet and Jackman on the 13th of July.—Ibid. p. 447,

Burrow, on the 21st of July.—Ibid. p. 277.

Governor Ellis, July 5th.—Voyage to discover the North West Passage, p. 127.

" The shores of Hudson's Bay have many inlets or friths, which are full of ice and snow, and frozen to the ground. These are broke loose, and launched into the sea, by land floods, during the months of June, July, and August."—Ibid.

" The first floating ice, which is observed on the coast of Labrador, is a joyful presage to the inhabitants of the approach of summer."—Lieutenant Curtis, in Philosophical Transactions,

" The ice begins to break up the 18th of June."—Danish Account of Greenland.—*Voyages au Nord*, vol. i, p. 167.

" The lakes of Lapland continue frozen on

June the 24th."—Linschoten's Voyage, ibid.
vol. iv.

" On the 5th of July, the sea on two sides
is observed to be covered with ice."—Ibid.
p. 187.

Wood sees the first ice in North Latitude
75° 59', on June 22.

On the 17th of August vast pieces of floating
ice.—Ibid.

" In the month of August the French observe, on the Labrador Coasts, mountains of
ice as high as the ships."—Boyle's Works,
vol. ii, p. 303.

" On June 16th, a river in Hudson's Bay
breaks up."—Mr. Wales, in Philosophical Transactions, vol. lx, p. 126.

" The mouth of the Lena is not open till
the middle of August."—*Observations Geographiques, par* M. Engel, p. 229.

With regard to the ice which may be observed in Southern Latitudes, I shall only

take notice, that Sir Francis Drake, Feuillee, and Clipperton, passed Cape Horn, or the Straits of Magellan, during the month of December, without mentioning ice*, from which it should seem that it breaks up chiefly during the months of January, February, and March, answering to our July, August, and September†.

Three Dutch Ships, which sailed on discoveries with Commodore Roggewein, in 1721, met with much ice to the South of Cape Horn in the middle of January. The Author of the Narrative afterwards makes this observation: " Those mountains of ice, which are seen in the latitude of Cape Horn, prove that there is land towards the Southern Pole, it being certain

---

* See Callander's Voyages under these three articles.

† It may possibly break up in some years earlier, perhaps in December; but some time must be allowed for its floating to the North, as far as the latitude of *Tierra del Fuego,* From the instances cited, it appears, that the earliest floating ice which is seen in the Northern hemisphere is not observed sooner than the 16th of June, whilst in much the greater part mention is not made of it till July.

that this ice cannot be formed in the ocean, though the cold is so severe*."

But it may, perhaps, be said, that the ice, which breaks up in June, July, and August, or during the correspondent months in the opposite hemisphere, may remain floating for years without being much dissolved.

To this I will not take upon myself to say that some such islands, when very large, may not continue more than a year; but I should conceive this not to be very common. Storms and other accidents must probably break them into small masses, which will quickly be thawed; as that able geographer and promoter of discoveries, Mr. Bailiff Engel, observes, that, if a piece of ice is fastened by a cord and let down into the sea, it is presently melted†.

Mr. Wales also informs us, that he supposes most of these islands of ice are soon wasted, in the following words: "The truth is, their

* *Histoire de l'Expedition de trois Vaisseaux, &c.* Hague, 1739, p. 81.
† See *Observations Geographiques,* p. 224.

motion and dissolution are apparently so very quick, that I am of opinion it must be a pretty large island which is not dissolved in one summer *."

How soon likewise does the ice disappear, which is discharged from our own rivers into the sea, after our most intense frosts?

I have omitted stating the degree of cold at which the sea water I exposed to the air began to be frozen, and cannot now recover the memorandum which I made at the time. I am pretty confident, however, that the mercury had sunk only to twenty-seven.

But though congelation thus took place at five degrees below the freezing point, it is proper that I should state some other circumstances attending the experiment.

The sea water which I used came from the North Foreland, which is at the mouth of the Thames, and consequently, not being the same with that of the ocean, was more easily frozen.

* Philosophical Transactions, vol. lx, p. 112.

Besides this, the quantity was so small as not to cover a thin china bason deeper than an inch, both which particulars contribute greatly to the more speedy formation of ice: it need scarcely be mentioned also, that the liquid to be frozen was in a quiescent state.

How much a considerable degree of motion impedes congelation, may be inferred from what may be observed in every river; for as high as the tide hath any force, I doubt much whether any ice is scarcely ever formed in the fair open channel, during our most intense frosts. I attended to the Thames, in this respect, during the late severity of the weather; and it seemed to me that all the ice floated down from the upper parts of the river; but packing afterwards between the lighters, occasioned the formation of very large masses.

I have little doubt, from these circumstances, but that the open sea, if it be frozen at all, must require a much more intense cold than twenty-seven; allowing however any greater degree of cold in the high latitudes, it seems deducible, from the experiments of Dr. Higgins, that sea water cannot be frozen into a solid state, if compared with that of ice formed from the water of rivers ; nor will such ice when melted become palatable, unless it hath been previously washed in fresh water.

Hence it seems to be almost demonstration, that the floating ice met with by navigators, being both solid and sweet to the taste after dissolution, cannot be produced from the water of the ocean *.

I will venture also to insist, that if such ice was actually frozen from the ocean, it must very quickly be melted, because, as it must consist of detached laminæ intercepting the brine, the sea would soon insinuate itself between the interstices, so as to cause its dissolution. If any ice, therefore, should be formed in those parts of bays which are land locked, have little

* The ice taken up by Captain Cook, during his circumnavigation in high Southern Latitudes, was solid and transparent ; being placed also on the deck for the salt water to drain off, the ice became wholesome and palatable water.

or no tide, and receive considerable quantities
of fresh water, when such ice is wafted fairly
out to sea, I should conceive that it must disappear in a very short time.

APPENDIX.

PAPERS

ON

APPROACHING THE NORTH POLE

AND ON

𝔄 𝔑𝔬𝔯𝔱𝔥 𝔚𝔢𝔰𝔱 𝔓𝔞𝔰𝔰𝔞𝔤𝔢.

BY

COLONEL BEAUFOY, F.R.S.

These Papers are extracted from Thomson's Annals of Philosophy,
by Permission of Colonel Beaufoy.

APPENDIX.

QUERIES

RESPECTING

THE PROBABILITY OF REACHING,

FROM

The Island of Spitzbergen, the North Pole,

BY MEANS OF

REIN DEER, DURING THE WINTER;

AND

ANSWERED

BY

PERSONS WHO WINTERED THERE.

SOME years past I was impressed with the idea of the possibility of reaching the North Pole from Spitzbergen, during the winter, by travelling over the ice and snow in sledges drawn by rein deer. Therefore, with the view

Q 2

of determining how far this plan was practicable, I sent several Queries, and requested Answers to them from Russians, who were at that time living at Archangel, and had wintered in those remote islands. Those Queries, together with the Answers, are as follow, as I learn from conversation that the practicability of such a journey, conducted in a similar manner, is entertained by well-informed persons; and, before a plan is put in execution, it is desirable to know what has been previously done on the same subject. The 31st and 33d seem contradictory, probably from some error in translating the Questions into Russ, or the Answers into English.

1. Query. How many settlements have the Russians on the island of Spitzbergen, and which is the most Northerly?

Answer. There are neither settlements nor fixed inhabitants in Spitzbergen, except those fishermen who go there in quest of fish, and likewise of those animals from Megen, Archan-

gel, Onega, Rala, and other places bordering
the White Sea, in vessels from sixty to one
hundred and sixty tons. They sail from the
above-mentioned places, those for the summer
fishery in the beginning of June, and those for
the winter in June and July. They arrive on
the West side of Spitzbergen, and commonly
return home, the former the same year in September, and the latter the next year in August
and September. They winter in the Gulphs of
Devil Bay, Clock Bay, Ring Bay, Crus Bay,
German Island, Magdalene Bay, and to the
Northward in Liefde Bay, and others. The
farthest North our fishermen ever have sailed
to is Liefde Bay, and from thence in small
boats as far as Nordoster Island.

2. Q. At what time of the year does the
winter commence?

A. The winter generally sets in about the
latter end of September and beginning of
October.

3. Q. Is it ushered in by storms? and is
any one wind particularly productive of them?

A. The winter sometimes sets in with

winds from the North, North North West, and North West; and sometimes commences with calm weather, hard frosts accompanied with snow.

4. Q. Is the weather, generally speaking, calm in winter, or are the winds high?

A. The winds are very high and frequent; so that two-thirds of the winter may be said to be boisterous.

5. Q. What quantity of snow do you suppose falls annually; that is, to what depth on the ground?

A. On even places the snow is from three to five feet deep; but the winds drive it from place to place, so as sometimes to render all passage impracticable; and on the coats between the hills there are mountains of ice, occasioned by the pressure of the waters and drift of snow.

6. Q. Are the storms of snow frequent, and of long duration?

A. The storms of snow are very frequent, continuing for two, three, and four days, and sometimes for as many weeks; but the latter do not occur above once or twice in a year.

7. Q. Is the cold much more severe at Spitzbergen than at Archangel ? Has the degree ever been ascertained by the thermometer? If it has, what was it?

A. From the fishermen's remarks, the cold is more severe at Spitzbergen than at Archangel; but the degree is not known, as the people who go there have no thermometers.

8. Q. Is the cold ever so intense as to render going abroad dangerous ?

A. The cold is never so severe as to hinder the fishermen, they being accustomed to it, from exposing themselves; but sometimes the winds and drifts of snow confine them to their huts.

9. Q. Admitting it to be so, by what exercise do the Russians keep off the scurvy ?

A. When the last mentioned weather is an obstacle to their leaving their huts, they keep off the scurvy by the exercise of throwing the snow from off and around their huts, which from stormy weather are often buried; and in order to get out, they are then obliged to make a passage through the roof. They likewise oppose the distemper by making use of a particular sallad or herb, which grows there on stones, and with which they generally provide themselves in due time against winter; but sometimes, from necessity, they are obliged to dig through the snow for it. Some of it they eat without any preparation; and a part they scald with water, and drink the liquid. They also carry with them for the same purpose, as a preventive, a raspberry, called in Russia *moroshka,* which they preserve by baking with rye flour, which they eat; and when pressed, drink the juice. They also take fir tops with them, which they boil; and the water they drink as an antidote likewise against the scurvy.

10. Q. In what manner are the huts constructed?

A. The huts the people use they always take with them in their vessels, and on their arrival there put them together. They are constructed of thin boards, and in the same

manner as the peasants' houses here. They
likewise generally take bricks with them for
building their stoves ; but when they fall short,
clay found there is made use of in their stead.
Their largest hut, which is erected in the
neighbourhood of their vessels, boats, &c., is
from twenty to twenty-five feet square, and
serves as a station and magazine; but those
huts the men erect who go in quest of skins
are only from seven to eight feet square, and in
the autumn are carried along the shores in
boats, and put up at distances from each other
of ten to fifty Russian versts. They take the
necessary provisions with them for the whole
winter to serve two or three men, as many
generally occupying each hut.

11. Q. What fuel have they, and in what
manner are their huts heated ?

A. The fuel commonly used for heating
their huts is wood, which they likewise bring
with them in their vessels, and land at the
station hut. In autumn the necessary quantity
for heating the aforesaid small huts is conveyed

in boats, or on small hand sledges, to the destined places. They often meet with wood there too, thrown by the sea on the shores.

12. Q. On what kinds of provisions do the Russians subsist during the winter?

A. The provisions they subsist on during the winter consist in rye flour (of which they make bread), salt beef, salt cod, and salted halibut, butter, oat and barley meal, curdled milk, peas, honey, linseed oil; all which they bring to Spitzbergen with them, and divide the same proportionally by weight to each man. Their employers allow them provisions for one year and a half, besides which the fishermen kill wild lion deer in winter, and birds in summer, which are experienced to be excellent food, and very healthy.

13. Q. Do they chiefly use spirituous or malt liquors?

A. They chiefly drink a liquor called *nuas*, made from rye flour and water. Malt and spirituous liquors are entirely excluded and forbidden by their employers, to prevent drunkenness, as the Russians, when they had it, drank so immoderately that work was often neglected entirely.

14. Q. When in the open air, how do they defend themselves?

A. They defend themselves from the rigour of the weather by a covering made of skin, above which they wear another made of the skin of rein deer, called *kushy*, and wear boots of the same.

15. Q. Do they not use masks, and omit the practice of shaving?

A. They use no masks, nor do they shave; but they wear a large warm cap, called *truechy*, which covers the whole head and neck, and most part of the face. They also wear gloves of sheep skin.

16. Q. Do the inhabitants cross the country during the winter?

A. There are no inhabitants, as said before; but the fishermen, who are there for a time, do go over from one island to the other of small distances.

17. Q. How do they travel, at what rate,
and how carry the necessary stock of provisions
for their subsistence during the journey ?

A. They travel on foot ; that is, on snow
skaits, and draw their food after them in small
hand sledges; but those who bring dogs with
them make use of the same. When travelling,
snow is their drink. Horses or rein deer would
be of no use to them for the conveyance of
their provisions ; nor have they any.

18. Q. By what means do they procure
water ; and is it by melting snow, or do they
find springs ?

A. They use spring water when it is to be
had, often take it from lakes, and from necessity sometimes dissolve snow ; but it seldom
happens that they are in want of fresh water,
because they commonly pitch on those places
where it is to be met with.

19. Q. Is not the ice so firmly consoli-
dated as to render all passage across it from
one island to the other perfectly safe during
winter ?

A. The ice at Spitzbergen is well conso-
lidated; and in some places the flakes run to
a great height, one on another, which makes
even the passage on foot very difficult; other
places are quite smooth, except those gulfs
which run in the land to about twenty versts,
where the ice is continually floating and drifting; but travelling with horses or rein deer is
quite impossible.

20. Q. Is not the ice rendered smooth by
the interstices being filled up with snow?

A. As before said, the ice is made smooth
by the snow filling up the inequalities.

21. Q. Does any danger arise either in
crossing the land or the ice, from the drifting of
the snow?

A. They do not journey in winter, as before mentioned, except to islands at trifling distances; and a traveller is in much danger if
surprised by a sudden gale of wind, accompanied by drifts of snow; he is obliged to lie
down, covering himself with his ———, and
remain so secured till the hurricane is over:

but when it continues for any length of time,
the poor wretch often perishes.

22. Q. What degree of light is there in
winter ?

A. The fishermen do not know what the
degree of light may be in winter; indeed, they
are ignorant of the meaning of the term : however, they say from the latter end of October to
the 12th of January the sun does not appear
above the horizon, which causes a continual
darkness, and obliges them always to keep a
light in their huts by burning train oil in
lamps; but as soon as the sun makes its appearance, the days increase very rapidly.

23. Q. What difference does the absence of
the moon occasion? Are the stars in general
brilliant? Can you see to read when the moon
is under the horizon ?

A. From the appearance of the moon in
her second quarter to her decline in the last,
the nights are very luminous, and the stars extraordinary light both day and night. In the
gloom of winter the people keep time from the

position of certain stars. When the moon is below the horizon, it is impossible to read.

24. Q. Is the Aurora Borealis very brilliant; and in what part of the horizon is it seen?

A. In the dark time of winter the Aurora Borealis is commonly seen most strong in the North, and appears very red and fiery.

25. Q. Does it appear possible to cross the ice in winter to the North Pole? If it does not, what are the obstacles?

A. The likelihood of a passage to the North Pole does not seem probable to the fishermen, as they have not had an opportunity to attempt it; and, from their observations, think all passage impossible, as the mountains of ice appear monstrously large and lofty. Some of the ice is continually drifting about; so that in many places water is discerned. Those who have been on the most elevated parts of Nordoster Island declare, that, as far as it is visible, open water is only seen; but to what distance it may continue so, it is impos-

sible for them to ascertain, as an attempt for
the discovery has never been made; but seem-
ingly it is practicable to bring the fuel and provisions in vessels to the Nordoster island.

26. Q. If the passage should be deemed
practicable, in what manner should it be attempted? and what means of conveying fuel
and provisions appear to be the best?

A. As the fishermen think all passage impracticable, it is not in their power to give any
answer to this demand.

27. Q. Might not three different huts, constructed like those in which the people of
Spitzbergen live, together with a sufficient
quantity of provisions in each for half a dozen
of people, be conveyed on sledges, and be left
at the different distances of two hundred, of
four hundred, of six hundred miles, North of
Spitzbergen, as places of deposit for the assistance of those who shall undertake the journey?

A. Such huts might be built, and placed
on shore, as said in the tenth article, at a convenient distance from their vessels; but as for

conveying them ready built to the distances proposed appears to the people an impossibility.

28. Q. What number of persons and rein deer, or of dogs, would be requisite for conveying the huts?

A. From the mountains of ice and great falls of snow, neither dogs nor rein deer would be able to draw loads; for the fishermen themselves, to be as light as possible, go on snow skaits.

29. Q. At what price per man for each day's journey would the people of Spitzbergen, if they think the adventure practicable, be likely to undertake the conduct of the sledges?

A. As, in the last reply, the fishermen show it is not convenient there to draw with dogs or rein deer, therefore no price can be said.

30. Q. Are there any persons in Archangel who have formerly resided in Spitzbergen who would engage in the business? and are there any who would be willing, in company with two Englishmen, to attempt on this plan a passage to the North Pole?

R

A. As there are not, nor ever were, any natives of Spitzbergen, none therefore can be resident in Archangel: however, many men may be met with here who have wintered there : but as they have never made an attempt to go to the Pole, they cannot undertake the conduct of the business. Notwithstanding, if an Englishmen should determine on the endeavour, some people might be met with who would perhaps, with an English ship's company, engage themselves.

31. Q. In the spring, have flights of birds ever been observed to direct their course North of Spitzbergen ?

A. It has been always experienced by those who have been at the most northerly parts of Spitzbergen, that in the spring a great number of wild geese, ducks, and other birds, take their flight farther North.

32. Q. What animals and birds have they during the summer, and what species winter on the island ?

A. In Spitzbergen they have wild rein-deer.

white and blue foxes, and white bears, which remain continually on the island ; but geese, ducks, &c., are only there in summer.

33. Q. Those which quit Spitzbergen on the approach of winter, in what month do they generally emigrate, and to what point of the compass ?

A. All the before-mentioned birds on the approach of winter, that is, in the latter end of September, fly to the Southward, and return again in the latter end of April.

N. B. The 31st and 33d Answers do not apparently agree.

THE NORTH WEST PASSAGE;

INSULAR FORM OF GREENLAND.

———————◆———————

THE reign of his present Majesty will ever be famous for the encouragement given to science; but in no branch has the King's gracious patronage been more conspicuous than in the discoveries made by different circumnavigators, especially by the immortal Cook. Considering the inducement and encouragement held out by our monarch for exploring the Northern Parts of the globe, and the number of ships annually fitted out from the different ports of the United Kingdom for Davis's Straits, Baffin's Bay, and Spitzbergen; it may appear very remarkable that no new discoveries are made, or old verified, or any voyage extended to a higher latitude than 81° North. The King's

wish of promoting discoveries in this part of the
world is evident from Lord Mulgrave's expedition, and more especially from the Acts of Par-
liament promising a reward of twenty thousand
pounds to any of his Majesty's subjects who
shall sail through any passage between the
Atlantic and Pacific Oceans to the Northward
of latitude $52°$ North, and also from a reward of
five thousand pounds to any British ship that
shall approach within one degree of the North
Pole. To what cause, then, can be attributed
the indifference and apathy of those commanders
of Greenland ships who, having been unsuccessful in the fishery, might be supposed to have it
in their power to defray the expense of the outfit
by sailing to the West or the North, with the
view of claiming one of the above rewards? It
cannot be said with justice that the masters of
our Greenlanders are either deficient in skill, or
indifferent to discovery; for among them, as in
other professions, men are found of superior
talent and of enterprising spirits. The paradox
will, however, be solved by referring to the sub-

joined oath*, which effectually excludes every conscientious person from endeavouring to carry into execution the scientific views of the Legislature in passing what may, without impropriety, be named the Discovery Act. When this last Act was passed, it is probable the former Act for promoting Northern discoveries did not occur to the framers. I remember some years past that a learned and scientific Member of the House of Commons was so much struck with the discouraging effect of the oath, that it was his intention to have brought forward a

* The following is a copy of the oath taken by the master, and also by the owner, of Greenland ships : — Master of the ship———maketh oath, that it is really and truly his firm purpose, and determined resolution, that the said ship, shall, as soon as license shall be granted, forthwith, proceed so manned, furnished, and accoutred, on a voyage to the Greenland Seas, or Davis's Straits, or the seas adjacent, there in the now approaching season to use the utmost endeavours of himself and his ship's company to take whales, or other creatures living in the seas, and on no other design or view of profit, in his present voyage, and to import the whale fins, oil, and blubber thereof, into the port of ———. Sworn at the Custom House."

clause enabling the masters of Greenland ships
to prosecute discoveries, as well as to catch fish ;
and it was owing to accident that a clause of the
above nature was not introduced. This omis-
sion, however, it is hoped, may yet be supplied
at no distant period, and Greenland voyages,
conducted as they are by seamen best qualified
for such an undertaking, be made subservient to
the exploring of the Northern Regions.

It may farther be observed, navigating among
the ice being in itself a science, men regularly
brought up to the sailing and working of ships
in the Arctic Circles should be selected for such
service, in preference to those accustomed to na-
vigate the more temperate parts of the globe.
It follows, therefore, that if at any future period
it should be the intention of Government to promote Northern discoveries, it would be advisa-
ble, both for economy and the greater probability
of success, to hire one of the Greenland vessels
and crew, sending on board as many scientific
and philosophical men as are deemed requisite.
The following statement was sent me some years

past by Captain Brown, an able and expert seaman, regularly brought up in the Whale Fishery, who was willing to undertake the exploring Baffin's Bay, or endeavouring to approach the North Pole. He mentioned, that, though in Baffin's Bay he had frequently run to the Westward, he had never got sight of land in that direction; which implies the Northern part of America may be much contracted. Brown, unfortunately, was killed at one of the Sandwich Islands :—

"SIR,   "*Jan.* 16, 1789.

"I shall begin fitting out the first of next month for Davis's Straits; and should you wish to explore Baffin's Bay, I shall be glad to have timely notice, that I may prepare a larger stock of provisions, provide presents for the Indians, and several other articles which will be necessary for that voyage. It will be proper for the bounty to be paid by the Treasury, or the Custom House Oath altered; and I think, when you peruse the subjoined account of expenses, you will not think my requisition of five hundred pounds per month, for two ships, extravagant. I only desire it to be paid from the time of leaving the fishery in 72° North till we return to Cape Farewell; and no payment to be made unless it shall satisfactorily appear the utmost has been done to explore Baffin's Bay, Lancaster Sound, &c. The expense Government would possibly incur would be very trifling; but as underwriters will not insure such voyages, the owners should be indemnified, and the value of the ships ascertained by the surveyor who values the transports, against the enemy, and other extra risks. I have perused all the Northern voyages, and shall perfect myself in lunar observations.

(Signed)   " WILLIAM BROWN."

THE NORTH POLE. 251

Ship Butterworth, three hundred and ninety-two *Tons**.
Boats, and forty eight *Men.*

		Per Month.		
		£.	s.	d.
1	Master	5	0	0
1	Surgeon	3	10	0
1	Chief Mate	3	10	0
1	Carpenter	3	10	0
1	Carpenter's Mate	2	10	0
1	Second Mate	2	10	0
1	Boatswain	2	10	0
1	Skim-man	2	10	0
1	Cooper	2	10	0
7	Harpooners at 50s. each	17	10	0
1	Cook	2	0	0
7	Boat steerers at 40s. each	14	0	0
7	Line coilers at 32s. 6d. each	11	7	6
17	Men at 30s. each	25	10	0
	48 Men's wages	98	7	6
	Men's provisions at 30s. each	72	0	0
	Wear and tear, 392 tons, at 5l. per ton	98	0	0
		£268	7	6

Cabin allowances, presents for Indians, extra liquor, and other encouragement for the people, cannot be estimated at less than 31l. 12s. 6d. per month, making a total of 300l.

Brig Lyon one-third less expense:

* A Vessel of the above tonnage with a rising floor is the best adapted for this service, as it has a sufficient momentum among the loose ice, and is easily managed.

As experiments are making on the length of
the pendulum in the Orkneys, it is highly desirable that scientific men be sent for the same
object in one of the Greenland ships to Spitzbergen ; and at the conclusion of the fishery they
might return in the same vessels.

Every Greenland vessel should be furnished
with an artificial horizon; of which the first
and best is a shallow cylinder of wood four
inches diameter in the clear, and three-tenths
and a half deep, into which, by means of an
ivory funnel, is poured quicksilver. To prevent the mercury from being ruffled by the
wind, two glass planes are placed over it,
whose surfaces are parallel, and forming an
angle with each other of 90°; and if this be
not sufficient protection when the mercury is
agitated by wind, or any heavy object passing
near, a circular piece of glass is floated on the
quicksilver. The second (invented, I believe,
by the late Mr. Adams, of Edmonton) is a
plane concave glass four inches in diameter,
and ground to a long radius. It is fitted into

a metallic box, with its concave side down-wards. This box, when wanted, is nearly filled with spirits, leaving a bubble; and by means of three screws, this bubble is brought into the centre of the glass. On one side of the box is a small thumb screw, to be taken out when filling, that the air may escape. This screw should not be made of iron, because it will corrode. If this instrument be well made, and pains taken in the levelling, it may be depended on to two minutes, which gives an error of one minute of altitude. Neither of these artificial horizons can be used when the altitude of the object exceeds 67°.

It would be extremely curious to ascertain the extent of the variation of the compass in Baffin's Bay. Captain Brown found it to be 79° 42′ West, in latitude 72° 46′ North (see the Annals of Philosophy, vol. vii, p. 14); and there being an increase from Cape Farewell to this latitude, it is not impossible, that in higher latitudes the augmentation may con-tinue, until the needle loses its polarity; which

extraordinary declination of the compass (pe-
culiar to this part of the world) is so remarkable, that, were a vessel sent for no other
purpose than of making magnetical observations, both the time and money which might
be bestowed on the expedition would be advantageously employed for the advancement of
science. The variation of the compass in latitude 70° 17′ North, and longitude 163° 24′
West, is 30° 28′ East; and in latitude 70° 58′,
and longitude 54° 14′ West, is 74° West;
whence it appears, that in nearly the same
parallel of latitude, and in a difference not
exceeding 109° 10′, or about one thousand six
hundred and eighty-five· geographical miles of
longitude, there is a difference in the variation
amounting to 84° 42′. It would also be a desirable discovery to ascertain whether on going
to the Westward it would be found that the
variation gradually decreases to the point of no
variation, and afterwards gradually increases;
or whether its return be not by a sudden jump
from West to East. Observations on points of

this description, accompanied with remarks on
the depth, temperature, and saltness of the sea,
and with a meteorological journal, would contain much interesting and valuable information,
and throw great light on the natural pheno-
mena of these unexplored regions.

The depth of the sea in Baffin's Bay has
been determined beyond doubt by Brown to be
more than a mile. It is not unusual in April
(the time the Greenland vessels arive in Davis's
Straits) for Fahrenheit's thermometer to stand
at 10° or 22° below freezing.

Considerable diversity of opinion prevails
respecting the form of Greenland, which is
conjectured by some to bend to the Westward,
and, joining the continent of America, to form
the vast and supposed gulf of Baffin's Bay; by
others, to be one large island ; and by a third
class, to be a cluster of islands intersected by
a variety of channels running from sea to sea,
but so blocked up with ice as to render the passage between them impracticable. In a journal
before me it is mentioned that a strong current

sets round Cape Farewell to the North West, and
that the water breaks for several miles. It appears probable, therefore, from this circumstance, that Greenland does not consist of a
multitude of islands; because in that case the
current would have taken its direction between
them, instead of flowing round the extremity of
the land. The junction of Greenland with
North America appears to me to be likewise
improbable, from the following reasons : first,
that Brown (as already mentioned) never saw
the Western land : next, that Hearn in his
travels arrived at the sea, seals having been seen
by him : and, thirdly, that Mackenzie, whose
travels lie to the Westward of Hearn's course,
came to the mouth of a large river, which also
emptied itself into the Arctic Ocean : and,
lastly, from the great probability that the immense quantity of drift wood found in Baffin's
Bay, on the Coast of Labrador, and on the
North West Coast of America, has been deposited there after being brought down by
Mackenzie's River, and driven to the East and

West, and afterwards Southward, according to the direction of the winds and currents : all which circumstances combine, in my opinion, to furnish a ground of belief that North, as well as South America, is surrounded by the ocean; and that the North West Passage is to be sought about latitude 72°. That Greenland is an island seems also to be highly probable, from the quantity of drift wood found on the Coast of Iceland; for it is much more natural to suppose the trunks of trees found in that part of the world are carried off from the Northern extremity of America, and driven round the North of Greenland, than that, being floated from the mouths of the Obi, Lena, and other great rivers of Russia, they should pass Nova Zembla, round the North Cape, to the prodigious distance of 20° West Longitude.

Cape Farewell, the Southern extremity of Greenland, according to the Requisite Tables, is in latitude 59° 38′ 00″ North, and longitude

s

42° 42′ 00″ West.   By observations in my possession, it is in latitude 59° 42′ North and longitude 45°, 16′ West.

T H E   E N D.

CHaRLES WOOD, Printer,
Poppia's Court, Fleet Street, London.

CPSIA information can be obtained at www.ICGtesting.com
Printed in the USA
LVOW13s0650060414

380405LV00001BA/82/P